Living in Uncertainty,
Living with Spirit

LIVING IN UNCERTAINTY, LIVING WITH SPIRIT

2nd Edition

JOHN C. WOODCOCK

iUniverse, Inc.
Bloomington

Living in Uncertainty, Living with Spirit

iUniverse books may be ordered through booksellers or by contacting:

iUniverse
1663 Liberty Drive
Bloomington, IN 47403
www.iuniverse.com
1-800-Authors (1-800-288-4677)

ISBN: 978-1-4759-5819-5 (sc)
ISBN: 978-1-4759-5823-2 (ebk)

Printed in the United States of America

iUniverse rev. date: 10/23/2012

CONTENTS

PERMISSIONS

Figure 10b. *Medusa*: by Nicholas Pioch @ http://en.wikipedia. org/wiki/file:medusa_by_carvaggio.jpg (Wikimedia Commons).

Figure 10c. *New Pieta:* personal photo of sculpture by Fenwick Lawson: http://www.fenwicklawson.co.uk/.

Figure 10d. *La Pieta (Michaelangelo)*: by Stanislav Traykov @ http://en.wikipedia.org/wiki/File:Michelangelo% 27s_Pieta_5450_cropncleaned.jpg (Wikimedia Commons).

Figure 10e. *Lascaux Cave Painting*: by Jack Versloot @ http:// en.wikipedia.org/wiki/File:Lascaux_II.jpg. (Wikimedia Commons).

Figure 10f. *Angelus Novus*: source: http://www.inicia.es/de/m_ cabot/paul_klee.htm @ http://en.wikipedia.org/ wiki/File:Klee,_Angelus_novus.png (Wikimedia Commons)

To my Woodcock ancestors who gave so much to me through the blood:

Gesta Verbis Praevenient

Perhaps you noticed it out of the corner of your eye—how even the most seemingly ordinary events can sometimes have such a significance that slip right through our awareness. And sometimes things can come to light, discoveries are made, that literally make no sense . . . The situation could be compared to thunder and lightning out in the countryside, so intense they can't be seen or heard: invisible lightning, silent thunder. Our minds simply won't acknowledge what's happened. And it's not only that everything seems to go on exactly as it did before; we're not even conscious of anything happening.

But there, where our awareness doesn't yet want to reach—that's where the future lies

Peter Kingsley: Dark Places of Wisdom

PREFACE

I n Bruegel's famous painting, *The Fall of Icarus*, our eyes are drawn to the "centre" of the world, where life goes on and where the *familiar* reigns supreme. Everyone is busy, heads down hard at work surviving or looking up, daydreaming what it must be like "up there"—you know, where we were we told the action is—*up there*! Simultaneously, an event of great spiritual significance occurs right in front of our eyes, not *up there* at all. And everybody misses it, intent as we are on our own busy-ness.

Bruegel painted (purportedly) this work in the 16th century. The fall of Icarus is pictured as occurring in the public domain as if to show that shared and direct sensual perception of spiritual events was still possible, or at least believed to be possible in the culture of that time. Spiritual reality was generally understood to be "near" ordinary reality. Owen Barfield points out (1988, 73) that angels portrayed in medieval art were clothed rather like ordinary people, with the addition of wings. Spiritual reality was believed to be, if not actually experienced as, "spatially" near and phenomenologically similar to the ordinary reality of the time.

We neither experience nor believe that this relationship of spatial proximity is true today. Spiritual reality and *our* ordinary reality are felt to be "far apart" having little or nothing to do with each other. Spiritual reality is not available to our sensual perceptions anymore, because our imagination and our ordinary sensual perceptions have become separated. We therefore are faced with an ordinary reality that is devoid of spiritual significance. To be sure, various art forms do from time to time depict angelic forms appearing amongst us, looking like us, as in the film *Michael*. But without exception, I think, the spiritual being so portrayed has to overcome sheer incredulity or worse, a deep cynicism in us modern humans against such appearances. Already in Bruegel's time a loss of direct spiritual perception was taking place, with an increasing spatial distance between ordinary reality and spiritual reality.

The loss seems complete now in the sense that we have created a culture in the West that proceeds pretty much as if there were no spiritual reality at all to take account of in our daily lives. We can't even intelligently point "up there" anymore because we know that there is only more matter up there, galaxies upon galaxies *ad infinitum*. If we were to ask where spirit is, we cannot point anywhere at all in spatial terms.

To highlight this enormous shift in our evolution of consciousness even further, consider the word *numinous*. This word conveys the meaning of an ordinary phenomenon appearing invested with a special charge of a normally invisible *presence*. Deep within this word is its Latin meaning—an image of a nodding head. It is not hard to imagine our ancestors taking careful notice when a statue of their god "nods" in assent, for example. This nodding was perceived and was thus available to their ordinary senses in a way that is not available to modern consciousness at all.

Our ancestors lived in a world that was saturated with spiritual significance. Spiritual reality was available to sensual perception through the agency of the *unusual* or the *unexpected*. For example, a startled horse would become the occasion for a concerned discussion about meaning. It was not a time to just go on, to return to the *familiar*, or to just "get on with it". People understood that an incursion had taken place from spiritual to ordinary reality and they sensually perceived it that way. Accidents or mishaps were not only *believed* to be occasions of such incursions. They were numinous events and were *perceived* that way.

Such thinking and perceiving can hardly be understood in modern culture's terms of reference at all. We are in such a frenetic rush that any unusual happening is almost despised. We have constructed some mighty fortresses—social structures such as insurance companies and indeed our legal system, for example, are designed to protect *victims* from the consequences of accidents or mishaps of any kind. The only kinds of attention we typically give to unusual events that disturb our routines are dismissive or aggressive as we seek only to maintain our lives, undisturbed by distractions of any sort.

Flat tires, ATM closures, Internet "downtime", lost credit cards, crashing computers, late buses, keys that don't work, stolen handbags, lost directions, bumbling bureaucrats, mislabelled consumer goods, software viruses, are all met with irritation, angry assertion of "my rights" and a conspiratorial rush to eliminate all evidence of the disruption to the other wise smooth operations of our lives. In this way we have successfully, and for many people finally and permanently, shut ourselves off from spiritual reality.

In shutting ourselves off from spiritual reality, our modern culture is left searching for *security* within present circumstances by means of constructed institutions such as health insurance, departments of homeland security, etc., and seeking *certainty* of the future in a similar fashion—superannuation funds, pensions, life insurance, etc. Ironically, we have instead constructed a culture of great insecurity (anxiety) and uncertainty (post-modernism).

Ours is a time of great uncertainty and insecurity in spite of the many structures we put in place to avoid feeling this way. Our insecurities flare up whenever an unusual event appears and cannot easily be dismissed or erased through such *apotropaic* means.

Living in uncertainty is *our* ordinary reality but do we need to live insecurely in this reality? Our insecurity stems from our separation from and denial of, spiritual reality. Henri Corbin calls this a double catastrophe! As he says it is one kind of catastrophe to realize that we have lost the keys to the kingdom of heaven. With this knowledge we at least can understand what our feelings of alienation are about and in a disturbing way a relationship to spiritual reality still remains. However, we have taken the further step of denying there is a problem, that our alienated condition is normal, to be treated with medications if it gets too bad. We have thus lost both the keys and any knowledge of lost keys. This is the double catastrophe for our modern culture.

I do want to avoid any suggestion that I am blaming our modern culture for such a catastrophe. Far from it! This outcome is consequence of the evolution of consciousness intersecting with our free will. The evolutionary fact is that we DO look out upon the surfaces of the world with sense perceptions that are stripped of spiritual significance. In so looking we also find ourselves as separate and conscious individuals. They go together!

The scientific way of thinking has succeeded mightily in separating our imagination from our senses. What was a titanic, conscious effort by the likes of Leonardo de Vinci and Galileo to distinguish and then separate (what came to mean) subjective from objective qualities of the world, has now become an unconscious *given* in all of us born subsequently. As we extracted subjective qualities from the world we gradually awakened to our individual self-consciousnesses and to a world bereft of spirit.

To be born in our times is to be born into the inevitability of an outer world devoid of spirit, with senses deprived of any imaginal qualities—those very qualities that give us the means of perceiving spiritual realities occurring in the world—*and* to be born as an self-conscious individual.

We *are* each responsible as members of our culture in the exercise of our free will. Where do we freely and wilfully choose to focus our attention in order to support our dominant interpretation of the evolutionary facts I spoke of above? Our dominant interpretation is that our spiritually bereft world surely exists now *and has existed this way for all time!* The corollary is that we have simply over time shaken off superstitions in order to come to know this fact.

I have examined the writing of many modern spiritually oriented people, major figures in the literature, and found to my astonishment that most simply accept this dominant theory of evolution as *fact!* They accept that earth has always been a material object in a universe of material objects separated from one another by empty space in which we are also placed as objects, except with growing self-awareness over time.

To support this evolutionary interpretation of our present reality we must, as free agents, hold our attention to certain phenomena while at the same time withhold our attention from other phenomena that would lead to alternative interpretations. Here are a couple of simple examples of this widely spread cultural process that effectively seals our doom as spiritual-sentient beings. If an unusual event occurs in my life, say, a car accident, I can interpret that event as an accident, a chance happening which by definition holds no meaning at all. So, the accident has nothing to do with my *being*. To be sure I can be held legally responsible but inwardly, as we all know, I can still cleave to feelings of victimhood, i.e., this event has nothing to do with *me*. My efforts are consequently directed towards reasserting the *status quo*. I seek apotropaic means of making the accident and its consequences disappear from my life, so I can return to normal.

Let's unpack some of the fundamental assumptions about self and the world from this all too common occurrence.

Within this occurrence, by an act of free will I have chosen to support the cultural belief that world is the result of random events colliding over time. Life is an accident "born" out of meaningless randomness. I chose to interpret the event as an accident, having nothing to do with me in the same way as the theory of evolution assures us, with great certainty, that our being born into the world is an accident, having no meaning because our birth is merely a small aspect of an evolutionary process that itself has no meaning.

In the same wilful way, I choose to withhold my attention from any aspect of the occurrence that would challenge such a bleak interpretation or would lead to an alternative one. Details possibly laden with spiritual significance and which indeed may be felt that way by individuals are thus lost because they are unsupported in cultural theory and individual interest. So, during the time of the accident, I may find myself strangely attracted to my adversary, a feeling that directly conflicts with my aggressive assertion of rights. In choosing to ignore the conflict in favour of my status as victim, I freely and wilfully end any chance of discovering the spiritual reality lying within or penetrating the surface event of an accident.

In these many small and fleeting ways, occurring throughout our days and nights, we deny spiritual reality and affirm the deadening cosmology that we are each born into today: a cosmology solely based on our relatively recent waking up to our self-consciousness *and* simultaneously waking to a world of surfaces, devoid of spiritual reality.

Our dominant theory of evolution asserts that the world always was the same "hard fact" (positive externality) and will ever be so. And by a systematic exercise of the free will given in self-consciousness we have constructed a culture that encourages, even demands its members fix their attention to phenomena that support the theory and to withhold their attention from phenomena that would challenge it in any way.

We may now well ask why anyone in their right mind would choose to help construct and/or support a culture that seeks to shut the door on any possibility of connecting with spiritual reality for its members as embodied sentient beings.

This question is worthy of a doctoral dissertation to be sure, at least. It is also a question that could be addressed to any proponent of the current theory of our origins, a theory that dominates all our educational institutions and as well the unconscious thinking of all individuals born into this culture. Political action is an appropriate form of action here and indeed conflicts are flaring up in the educational scene of the USA with the current theory of evolution being challenged by proponents of Intelligent Design for example. It is not difficult to discern within these dog-fights a deeper political agenda in which the religious "right" is vying for political power at the national level with the "leftist" liberals who are running the show within the Academy. However appropriate and timely such action may be, not all of us can engage in such actions and so what else can we do?

This book is therefore directed to those individuals who sense that there is significance to their lives not being addressed by our culture's "official narrative". It is also directed to those who feel empty, anxious, guilty, lost, or seeking, i.e., who feel themselves to be *of* a spiritual nature and yet who have been born into a spiritual wilderness when they look through their senses at the world around them.

I can show here in this book my own attempt to deal with emptiness, despair, and a sense of being alien to the world rather than belonging to her. I hope to show how one man lives in uncertainty yet lives with spirit.

INTRODUCTION

As modern beings, we are born into our own times and are bound by the necessities of our time, just as our ancestors were. We are born into a time when an acute self-consciousness coupled with a world bereft of spirit is the evolutionary necessity.

I am quite aware that there are remarkable people who are born into our times with clairvoyance, a given ability to perceive spiritual reality appearing through the senses, "out there" in the world. These people often become spiritual leaders, reminding us of the spiritual reality from which we have been so ineluctably separated. They try to teach us how to return to this reality using methodologies that were developed in the past, often remote past. They successfully awaken a longing in us for that spiritual reality that is indeed our origin (though not according to our current cosmology which is based on a purely materialistic evolutionary theory—from dead matter to life, etc.)

Sadly, poignantly perhaps, what was given to us freely in the past (clear spiritual perception) has been withdrawn and there is no return for the modern mind. At best the modern mind can "play act" clairvoyance, or imagine as if certain spiritual realities were seen outside as *the world*. Even when an authentic spiritual vision is granted to the non-clairvoyant, it fades and the individual is left once again feeling separate from just about everything, including that wonderful vision that seemed for a while to change everything.

To proceed towards the unknown future, we moderns must answer a couple of culturally significant questions. We are told by our dominant theory of origins (see Preface) that the world we are born into, and look out *upon*, is the same world that existed for all time—a collection of material, discrete objects that are separated in an empty space and we are part of that collection. This dominant theory has worked its way into our language and culture so deeply now that it has become an inveterate habit *in our daily conduct*. We daily act as though it were true, with no other possibility considered.

We can each easily accept the *now* part of the theory on the basis of immediate experience. The real world does indeed appear before our senses as a collection of sharply defined discrete objects in otherwise empty space. This is coupled with the equally verifiable fact (verified on the basis of immediate experience) that we each are individual consciousnesses, separated from that world and one another through space, like any other material object.

So the first question we can ask concerns the *then* part of the theory. *Were we and the world in this separated condition for all time in the past?* There is a great and urgent cultural debate offering on this question. I won't enter it here but instead I will press on to my own answer.

No, it wasn't!

During the course of this book, I hope you will find out how I came to this deeply felt and verifiable conclusion. For now, let us press on to the next question: if the world and human consciousness were in a different relationship in the past (as I now assert without proving), one that present-day clairvoyants are pointing us to, then what is the evolutionary task associated with our times, having arrived at a condition of maximum separation, looking out on a world of surfaces bereft of spirit?

My own answer is one that drives my work in the world today. Our modern "evolutionary task" is two-fold: We must first awaken completely to the existential fact of our separation from the world, which fact brings with it several gifts: feelings of enormous anxiety, inexplicable guilt, deep pervasive grief, and clear knowledge of a newly won freedom to choose. All these gifts come together in one package! From this stark fact we can work towards the exercise of free choice through an act of will to participate in the creation of a culture that reflects a transformed version of the world we were freely given in previous times, i.e., a world infused with spiritual reality. The clairvoyant experiences a world whose dominant creative power is love. This reality is *given* to the clairvoyant. The modern individual must *re-create* it, but not in an atavistic sense. We must create it *out* of our state of alienation from spiritual reality through a voluntary act of free will.

What would such a task look like when taken on by modern individuals? What would a world transparent to spiritual reality look like today? And what kind of individual would be formed in so experiencing the world this way?

My book is a series of essays that describe how one modern individual takes on this modern task. I face the fact of being a modern ego looking out on a world bereft of spiritual reality. I reject the dominant idea that this condition has been so for all time. I participate in the "evolutionary task" of forming a world that is material *and* spiritual, available to our transformed senses, in immediate experience.

These essays are descriptions of actual experiences I had while engaging in my task. They show how the world begins to transform as the senses themselves transform. They show glimpses of a new world that begins to show her face to us as we undergo the necessary alchemy to perceive her, once created anew. This new world is formed as governed by the dominant principle of *interpenetration* in contrast to our current world governed by its dominant reality principle of *disjunction*.

To give a taste of what is to come I will now relate one small incident that occurred in my life as I entered my "evolutionary task" (taken from my essay, *Year of the Peacock*):

I had been fired only that afternoon. An administrator from the head office called me on the phone and told me to come to headquarters where he would give me my severance pay and my marching orders. I was not to return. I asked if I could go to my office to collect all my belongings including an extensive sand tray collection of miniatures. I was a therapist working with abused children. He agreed to that request and an hour or so later I turned up at his door. He led me to me to a large empty conference room where he sat at the head of a long table and I sat somewhere towards the middle. Without any explanation he shoved an envelope stuffed with dollars and got ready to get up. I was filled with anxiety as I did not have a clue why I had been fired. My mind was racing as I tried to find a reason myself and I felt aggressive towards his alpha-male approach to my difficulty. I asked him why and true to form he gave me administrative babble: "Oh we are just doing a reshuffle of staff at the office . . .", etc. His lying cover-up was transparent to me and I became quite angry inside.

Right at that moment, I glanced out the door. You see, there was a door open to a rather lush English garden. Just as I was about to launch an attack, a most beautiful peacock strolled past the door. A *moment* had arrived! Something unusual happened. Something intruded in on the familiar scene of my being rejected, having the truth withheld, etc. I now had a choice as a free individual. And I *felt* the freedom in that moment. I could have easily ignored, dismissed, or erased the presence of that peacock and return to the familiar world of separation (e.g., me and the administrator) or I could step into my task of participation with a new world, with all the consequences that follow . . .

I turned to my adversary and said, "A beautiful peacock, do you have many here"? He laughed and said, "Yes, when they call out like that we think it is children screaming".

And so the moment passed. I simply picked up my severance pay and said goodbye. I felt quite calm and in a strange way reconciled with the decision to fire me. A strange and unfamiliar meaning had intruded at just the moment I was going to let fly with my anger but instead focussed my attention on the unusual event of the appearance of the peacock. I listened and so did the administrator. What we each heard taught me that we belonged in different worlds. I had no part to play in his and he knew nothing about mine. The peacock with its strange uncanny, piercing voice was quickly assimilated by the administrator to his familiar world: a world in which the children are screaming.

He of course heads an agency that intends to do something about that screaming, not noticing that he becomes blind to anything else the children may be doing, such as getting better. In this way so many institutional structures perpetuate themselves at the expense of the very individuals they intend to serve.

On the other hand I heard a *call*. I did not know the meaning of the call but I knew it to be one. I felt pulled by that call and my familiar world of feeling victimized and aggressively defensive dropped away. Most importantly, *I acted on the basis of that call*. I shook the administrator's hand and walked into the unknown future. I knew where I did not belong and I stepped into uncertainty. On the basis of immediate experience, I felt the spiritual reality that infused the moment with the peacock and I answered the call.

I had a moment of great uncertainty and I lived a moment with spirit.

AUGURY OF THE CROW

I was walking along to the final class I would ever teach at Antioch University. I passed some trees where I heard a young crow cawing loudly. It was early summer so I assumed he was calling for his mother to feed him. I watched for a while and then moved on, intent on getting to class. The little crow hopped from tree to tree in the street along with me. I slowly grew interested enough in his behaviour to forget that I was moving until I jammed my knee into the nearest fire hydrant that could find its way towards me.

OK OK I'll watch where I'm going!

But the little bird continued along with me. So I stopped, and decided to experiment. I walked back along where I had come. He followed me. I resumed my way towards school and so did he, cawing loudly and insistently. When I stopped, he stopped, never ceasing his call. I went inside a building for a while and there he was waiting for me when I came out, resuming his flight along side, following me and cawing as I made my way to class. By now it HAD become "He was following me and was calling to me". The experience had quite definitely become that now.

I felt a peculiar feeling, a tension growing in my belly as we went on. I ducked into a shop to get him some food but he ignored it, perching on a building ledge cawing at me. I then saw his mother flap down beside him with some food for him but he ignored the offering, preferring, it seemed, to call at me.

I started to gather a strong feeling that something was urgent in this, that I was not getting it, that he was trying to get something through to me and I had yet to get it. I felt quite nervous and a heightened sense of alertness gathered around me.

I still had thirty minutes before class so I quickly went upstairs to my room and turned all the lights off so that I could crawl into a corner and see what would happen next. Well, I immediately looked out the window and there he was, my little crow, calling me, his whole body opened to the effort of . . . what? I could no longer shake the conviction that he was trying to get something through to me and that I had to make an effort to find a way to reach him, to understand him.

Obviously I was not going to do it with my egoically. I had to find another "place" where we could communicate . . . just had to! I was fully engaged now. I felt an imperative not to leave this experience without success. My little crow's urgent cries were unnerving me. I felt highly attuned to him.

I let go!

Immediately, I recalled a passing moment, earlier in the day:

I am walking to my office when I pass a second-hand book store. An artist is parked just outside in his customary place where he copies famous paintings onto his canvas. However, it is not him this time. Another artist is there painting birds, not copying them, but drawing from his own interior instead. I pause. He is in casual conversation with an elderly lady, a tourist, so I fancy. He tells her, and by the subtle method of eavesdropping while pretending to do something else, he also tells me that birds have to cock their heads side by side in order to get a whole picture of something. He goes on to say that birds, having eyes opposed, one on each side of their head, cannot easily form a whole picture of what they see. They see two distinct pictures that cannot be made into a whole.

As this memory surfaced, another was quickly released. In Melville's book *Moby Dick* there is a passage where Melville describes the whale's head, with its little eyes: [1]

> *. . . the whale, therefore, must see one distinct picture on*
> *this side and another distinct picture on that side; while*
> *all between must be profound darkness and nothingness*
> *to him.*

(Ch.74)

Then he poses a question whether the whale can simultaneously attentively examine two distinct prospects, one on each side of him. He notes that whales sometimes behave as if they are reacting helplessly to two distinct events which are acting upon them through their diametrically opposed eyes.

From these recollections, I remembered a puzzling passage I had read in Jung's *Zarathustra* lectures, where he equates the symbol of the eagle with the brain of man. [2] The wings correspond to the two halves of the brain while the body corresponds to the commissure, where the two halves meet and communicate with one another. Jung refers to this organ as the seat of consciousness, where the naïve mind experiences oneness, never realizing or feeling at all the two halves on either side of that seat.

Even now as I write, yet another memory is released. I saw a film long ago in an undergraduate psychology class where experiments were carried out on the consciousness of people who had had the two halves of the brain separated by surgery. They could function perfectly well except in circumstances where contradictions arose. It seemed that each half carried on as if it had absolutely no knowledge of the other half at all.

As these memories were released I wondered if there were something about all this that I needed to get. What would the "bird" need from the human that is connected to the bird's

---

[1]   (Melville, 1980)

[2]   (Jung, 1988)

structure of the eye and brain, or the whale's and the human's brain structure? Does he need me as the human to do something that he cannot do? Does he sense the urgency, the imperative of getting it done yet needing the human representative to carry it out?

I felt and still feel very disinclined to treat this experience with the little crow as a projective field in which I might explore a purely human psychic matter such as the bird representing some aspect of my human psyche, etc. Rather it feels to me to be the world calling me through the mouth of this little crow, seeking to connect with me on a matter of vital urgency, requiring my immediate attention.

I regard the place where I found those memories as precisely that place where the human, the animal and the world meet and can speak the same language. It is in this sacred place where creation can meet and speak to its human representative. Yes, there is work for me to do now that I have received the sacred speech. I feel a strong sense of responsibility towards my little friend the young crow and through him, all of creation. I desire somehow to bring this sacred speech into the world, so that others may hear it. It is early days for me—just two months after my encounter but I have begun to weave this experience into a whole web of connections that have presented themselves to me over the past few years (early 1990s).

Clearly it has something to do with the problem of the opposites, which is the theme of the entire *Pisces* Eon. This problem is captured symbolically in the mythic conflict between the eagle and the serpent, with the *Piscean* solution of the eagle's overcoming the serpent, or spirit overcoming matter. As I said, Jung likens the eagle to the function of human brain as experienced from within. I take this to mean that when the serpent is overcome then we are left with a consciousness that is certain of its oneness and blinded to the two opposing halves that lie to the side and beyond its range of vision, informing it perhaps in a determinative manner, totally outside consciousness.

As Jung states in *Zarathustra*, from the psyche's point of view it's not that the problem of opposites is ever solved. Rather, the nature of the problem shifts. Discrimination followed by moral evaluation of the opposites is the *Piscean* problem. Reconciliation of the opposites in a way that does not morally evaluate one or other of the opposites is the *Aquarian* problem.

I began to imagine my little crow as having a "bird brain", two halves that cannot unite in consciousness and the human as having that place where this bird brain can unite itself in consciousness. And there seems to be something very urgent about this. It's not so much a problem of the human uniting something within, as a separate matter from the rest of the world. A real living bird as *other* had approached me with his plaintive cry, after all. And as I said, the experience did not carry the qualities of a projected human content.

I am left with questions that direct me to the future.

Creation is suffering and calling to the human for help. What is the suffering? Can I feel my way into the bird, becoming the crow, looking out on the world from the point of view of the crow? Can I go to the whale, immersed in the waters?

The Age of *Aquarius* is an age of the human who carries the water, is not immersed in it like the whale. So it is the human to whom the bird turns now, not the fish. Perhaps the fish (whale) turns to the human too. Is there something about the human that creation needs and needs urgently to redeem creation from its suffering? Does this suffering have to do with a struggle to become conscious of itself? Does it need the human to help by *becoming* the world, by voluntarily ending his separation from the world and entering *into* it with his unique psychic structure which can thus help creation achieve its goal?

Why the crow? Some birds do have front-on vision but maybe the issue is to do with perception and the effect of opposites appearing simultaneously? Why the whale? The whale's eyes excited Melville's imagination to the problem of the determinative power of opposites impinging simultaneously on the organism. Bird, whale, and the human being!

Suppose the divine mind is in two halves which are trying to unite in order to make consciousness (probably the greatest mystery of all) so that it can experience itself in time and space. It therefore creates organisms to help: birds, whales, etc., and finally humans with a commissure, the means by which Creation's original unity may be restored in the incarnate state.

LIGHTHOUSE AT THE END OF THE WORLD

I n 1997, I entered a Ph.D. program. This step was based on highly unusual and improbable events that had accumulated around me, acting as a sort of funnel into the future. I had no money and all other options seemed closed to me. I was despairing of my life which had been stripped down to the bone in order that I might participate in the incarnation of certain ideas that penetrated my being through the unconscious. A friend gave me the admissions brochure three times over a month and finally I accepted it, wrote out an application, and paid with a credit card. I had no idea how I would finance the program and indeed how I would even pay to get to the colloquium or buy a book.

I was accepted, although the school did send me to a psychologist who checked me out to see if I was stable enough to last the distance. My thesis concerns the phenomenon of the end of the world. It was to be a heuristic study, since I was proposing to research what I myself had undergone: an apocalypse. I proposed that the end of the world theme in literature and in actuality could be explored as a phenomenon that occurs in the transformation of the individual as much as that of the world.

The course of my program, and its eventual outcome was not planned by me in advance at all. It unfolded as I undertook the task (see Introduction) of paying attention to unusual events that penetrate my consciousness, then acting upon my experience. The single most significant event that steered me towards my goal was a dream in 1997, prior to my entering the program.

I visit Anita and she tells me she is dying with cancer, a very tender, very sad moment. We go to a busy bookstore where she breaks down and tells me that she has never

been able to read books because she has never been able to
find a still place inside. She has a boy friend that becomes
threatening at one point. I see a lighthouse at the end of
a long narrow peninsula and I feel excited about it. We
must go visit it, I say.

A few days after this dream as I browsed through an online
bookstore, I was startled to find a book called *The Lighthouse
at the End of the World* by Stephen Marlowe. I immediately
thought of my dream lighthouse at the end of a long peninsula.
The synchronicity brought together lighthouses, books and the
end of the world. I remembered also that Anita was raised as
a Seventh-Day Adventist. This religious denomination bases its
spiritual guidance on *Revelation* and is centrally concerned with
apocalyptic wisdom.

I began to feel that "something" in my life was gathering
momentum. I felt a hidden significance to these events and they
produced a moral response in me. I felt I needed to become
attuned to these images, to synchronize my movements somehow
to these hints.

I went shopping for Christmas and noticed a model
lighthouse staring at me. I bought it. I was presented with a
Christmas gift of a lighthouse calendar and on the Internet I
found a lighthouse at Sequim, quite near where I lived. To get
there, visitors must travel to the end of a long sandy peninsula,
as in my dream. After a movie one night soon after, a friend
and I drove through the city and became lost. It was very late at
night and we were running low on gas. I turned a dark corner
in an area of town under the freeway and there in the middle
of the familiar waterfront buildings was a life-size replica of
a lighthouse, fully lit up, indeed a beacon in the dark night.
Soon after returning home, I consulted the *I Ching* and received
the hexagram for *The Wanderer.* The last line said: "Maintain
your integrity! It may become your lighthouse in the sea of the
unknown".

Something was approaching me from the world through these unusual events and I did not need any more hints to pay close attention. I eagerly awaited the book that in one image combined all the hints that I had received: lighthouses, the end of the world, and books. But I was still quite unprepared for what came next. When I received the book I was immediately gripped by the synopsis on the fly-leaf which described the book as an exploration of the convergence of two realities. This is close to the language I was using to formulate the phenomenology of the end of the world. I was proposing that the experience of the end of the world in contemporary times is one in which the Cartesian paradigm, based on a principle of *separation of realities* is being transformed into a new paradigm, based on a principle of *interpenetration of realities.*

I was equally startled by the fact that the book was based on the life of Edgar Allen Poe.

Poe was a childhood hero of mine. I had his collection of *Tales of Terror* and read them eagerly over many years—*The Pit and the Pendulum, The Maelstrom,* and *The Fall of the House of Usher* being my favourites. Poe is unrivalled as an artist expressing the form of literature known as Gothic Romance. I also had rediscovered him more recently in connection with another dream that had announced to me: "Your life is a High Gothic novel!" (see essay, *From Dream to World*).

My own life, the Gothic imagination with its focus on the end of civilization through the eruption of the powers of chaos or forces of irrationality and my work on the phenomenon of the end of the world, were all now linked in my imagination with the life and work of Edgar Allan Poe to whom I had been magnetically drawn as a child.

There was more to come . . .

My research into Gothic literature intertwined with yet another thread involving the symbols of the peacock, its connection to the comet, its role in my own life and the phenomenology of the end of the world (see essay *Year of the Peacock*). So I became speechless when I opened Marlowe's book to Page Two and found the fictional Poe narrating his confusion about the (historically factual), missing five days of his life, just before he died: [3]

> Where had I gone, those five days? And what done? And in whose company? I had been on binges before. Surely that was the sum and substance of it, a not very mysterious mystery. But then why, in hospital, in what little remained to me of afterwards, did I sometimes call myself Mr. Peacock?*

There was an asterisk and so I looked down to the footnote and read:

> It cannot be said with any certainty whether or not Mr. Poe knew that the word for "peacock" in Old Norse is poe.

So now, two more threads in what seemed to be an increasingly complex fabric began to weave together. And yes, throughout Marlowe's book there is a major role given to comets and the end of the world! As I continued my examination of Marlowe's book I found a chapter which opened with Poe heading out to a lighthouse on a desolate island. He is trying to finish a book that had eluded him. In fact a footnote told me that when the historical Poe had died, he had left fragments of a book that was called: *The Lighthouse at the End of the World*. This was a thrilling discovery for me and I began to feel a weird sense that my life and Poe's were intertwined in some way that involved Gothic romance, peacocks, comets, lighthouses and the end of the world. I read on:

> His unstrung nerves were, of course, what had brought Edgar there, two hundred miles from the nearest land . . . His unstrung nerves were why he

---

[3] (Marlowe, 1996)

had been unable to finish the most ambitious work he had ever undertaken, a novel, as yet untitled, about the end of the world. Although the last few chapters remained to be written, he had not set pen to paper for months. In that time the insidious idea grew that, possibly, the story had no ending. Was it too apocalyptic? Or too far beyond his imaginative powers? It had come to obsess him, to consume his every thought, his every waking hour. He drank little, ate less. He avoided social contact, persuading himself that that was the real problem, that people insisted on bedeviling him with talk, talk and more talk, when he craved the silence to immerse himself in the ending of the work he could not finish. Soon he began to dream of a writer, rather like himself, who was obsessed by a story he was struggling—with what desperation Edgar well knew—to finish; a story about the end of the world. His dream-self, deciding that isolation was the answer, sought employment as a lighthouse keeper. (207)

I certainly could feel the relevance of his anguish over writing and finishing his book as my own in trying to give voice to my ordeal that had lasted for nearly twenty years. I eagerly turned to the beginning of the book and began to read. The structure of the book expresses an increasing complex interpenetration of dream, waking life, the fictional Poe and the historical Poe. It felt so much like the unfolding of my own life that I felt unnerved. Inner and outer, self and other, past present and future, were in such close proximity, so relativised and intertwined, that the book approached an experience of madness that I knew so well. Marlowe portrays an uncanny interpenetration of realities that are normally kept apart, within a deeper context of an apocalypse brought about by a comet. As I read on I felt a frightening sense of dissolving structures just as Emerson describes it in *The Over-Soul*:

> *The things we now esteem fixed shall, one by one, detach themselves, like ripe fruit, from our experience, and fall. The wind shall blow them none knows whither. The landscape, the figures, Boston, London, are facts as fugitive as any institution past, or any whiff of mist or smoke, and so is society, and so is the world. The soul looketh steadily forwards, creating a world before her, leaving worlds behind her. She has no dates, nor rites, nor persons, nor specialties, nor men. The soul knows only the soul; the web of events is the flowing robe in which she is clothed.*

Marlowe's story shows a collapse of fixed structures based on opposites, leading to an apocalypse. He created a fictional Poe who intersected with the historical Poe as if to stress that fiction and history can no longer be kept apart either.

A lighthouse at the end of the world! "Maintain your integrity—it may become your lighthouse in the sea of the unknown". A lighthouse: a place at the edge of the known universe sending out a light into the blackness of the abyss; a place at the edge, bleak, desolate, lonely, barren and dangerous—where sanity itself is tested; integrity as a lighthouse—able to withstand the storms of an apocalypse and at the same time, being a beacon of light.

My friend has a book on the table. My eyes widen for it is called *House of Light,* a collection of poems by Mary Oliver. [4] I tell her my tale of lighthouses and of course, she gives me the book as a gift. I open it at random and find the *The Buddha's Last Instruction*: "Make of yourself a light". Ahh! Yes! The *I Ching* had also instructed me and what was that dream I had, so many years ago?

> *I am sitting at a table. A huge wind begins to buffet me. I start shaking as it gets stronger. I reach out and grab my*

---

[4]　(Oliver, 1990)

*mani stone which is sitting at the centre of the table and
begin to chant Om Mani Padme Hum—praise to the jewel
at the heart of the lotus—as the wind reaches a crescendo.
I hear in the background a group of Tibetan monks
supporting me, chanting too. The stone, the chant—I hold
together. The wind abates. I have survived. The wind had
pervaded my body and leaves me now with the ambiguity
of whether the wind was a subtle one or my body had
become more subtle. There had been an interpenetration
of realities! I remembered how, in previous dreams I had
simply been blown away like a leaf, by these storms.*

Edgar Allen Poe died at the age of 40. He lived on the edge and
was assailed by the storms of the abyss:[5]

*Waves broke like thunder against the lighthouse, which
seemed—was it possible—to sway . . . White water
surged from all sides, submerging the base of the tower.
The lenses of the lamp, opaque with streaming water,
stared sightlessly out at the raging sea. For forty-eight
hours, except for the wind and the surf, a world outside
the walls of the lighthouse ceased to exist. And then it was
over . . . Edgar prowled the living quarters until dusk . . .
In the clockworks room once more, Edgar swiftly wrote
"The Lighthouse at the End of the World", and in the
solitude resumed at last to write. (212-213)*

Having survived the storm, he prepares to send a shaft of
light out into the growing darkness . . .

*   *   *

Near the autumnal equinox of the year, late at night, I
pack the last of my possessions into the car. I have released my

---

[5]   (Marlowe, 1996)

connections to Seattle and am about to journey across the plains of Montana and North Dakota in order to join my fiancée in Michigan, a mid-western state that I know nothing about.

Floating easily at 80 mph on the thin ribbon of road that stretches across the prairies I am reminded of my solitary motor bike journey across Australia so many years ago, just before my coming here to the USA. That journey had been a prelude to an enormous leap into the abyss. I had left my beloved Anita behind in Sydney, the very same Anita whose image appeared in my dream. As soon as I had reached the USA, I began a spiritual ordeal that was to span 20 years.

I wonder if this move will carry similar consequences.

My journey is uneventful and free. I feel as though with each passing mile old skins are shedding off my back and that I am being newly born. The expanse of grassy plains is replaced by the farming fields and ponds of Minnesota until in the early pre-dawn, the time of Sophia, I arrive at the gray morning border of Michigan. I decide to go to the rest stop that is there to welcome tourists.

As I pull in to the parking area, I see a large shape emerge from the darkness. I am tired and feel inclined to ignore the lighthouse that appears, towering over me. Perhaps I am also a bit habituated to yet another one arriving spontaneously into my experience. But then I am jolted into alertness: A lighthouse! What the hell is a lighthouse doing here at a tourist welcome centre, in Michigan of all places?! I get out of my car and go quickly over to the lighthouse to read the plaque nearby. To my complete astonishment I learn that Michigan is the state of lighthouses—hundreds are preserved around its lakes and the state uses a lighthouse logo, so proud it is of these legacies.

Now I know that my arrival here in Michigan carries my destiny and that there is an interpenetration of worlds at hand. My dream has steered me to this state of lighthouses where I am indeed to learn how to be a lighthouse in a storm that was to last five more years, taking me once again to the edge of madness.

YEAR OF THE PEACOCK

I n 1987, I found a picture that helped save my life. It came from a series of plates in *Splendor Solis* by Salomon Trismosin, showing the stages of transformation in the alchemical opus. In this picture there is: [6]

> . . . *a sealed vessel within which is a fiery dragon tended by a naked child or homunculus. In the child's right hand is a bottle from which he is pouring water down the dragon's throat. In his left hand is a bellows with which he is fanning the flame. The text speaks of opening the holes and cracks of the earth "to receive the influence of Fire and Water". The picture illustrates the operation of the opposites, fire and water being applied simultaneously. This is exactly what happens to Tantalus; his desire is simultaneously inflamed and extinguished. The primitive, desirous aspect of the transpersonal psyche collides with the spiritual principle of restraint and self-denial, and Tantalus becomes a living crucible for the transformation of God.* (101-102)

This picture and the meaning it conveyed symbolically spoke directly to my heart. Two principles, two worlds in conflict appear within the one body. The picture portrays the most extreme tension between opposites—fire and water—and the impossibility of their union. Yet such a transformation IS possible. Transformation! Where I had only felt the immediacy of sheer survival from one moment to the next, I now had a clue

---

[6]   (Edinger, 1984)

that there is intentionality, a hidden purpose working behind the scenes. My own ordeal is connected to a transformation of some sort. What is being transformed and into what? The text said that God is being transformed and according to the alchemical sequence, He is being transformed from a dragon of desire and fear into what? The answer was found in the last of a sequence of four pictures which shows a peacock in full display standing proudly in the retort.

A few years later, I was fired from my agency job where I worked with children, using the sand tray method. The dismissal was sudden, and without explanation. I met with the administrator and as he was telling me the usual bureaucratic mumbo jumbo as to why I was fired, I saw three peacocks just outside the door quietly looking in. I quietly interrupted him, pointing them out. Without shifting his momentum he said that they are noisy birds and when they cry out he and others think it is children screaming. As he spoke, I was reminded of a dream I had of a client of mine who was in desperate straits. In the dream I place her in a tent and I lay bread crumbs at the entrance to attract the peacocks that would heal her . . .

When I left the office the peacocks were gone but I felt this experience held much meaning—that is, the firing, the appearance of the peacocks and the sudden eruption of my dream memory are threads to a weaving of some kind.

The most immediate effect of this event was to separate me from the mental health profession. The peacock experience was a *moment*. It revealed the nature of the mental health profession and my relationship to it. The administrator's response to the appearance of the peacock was to assimilate the fresh experience to the screams of children. That is all he and the profession can hear. It is reductive and keeps the industry going. I don't belong there. His response neglected the moment of the peacocks arriving at the door and instead he spoke about screaming children, i.e., his own fixed categories into which all direct experience is pushed. The peacock became screaming children. My response was more immediate and I did not assimilate the moment to my feelings of being fired. For example, I did not conclude that the peacocks were protesting the firing.

Instead it felt more like an appearance, at the very moment that I was being booted out of a job and indeed as it turned out, from the entire Managed Health Care system. In other words, as I was being led away from collective containers of experience, something was coming towards me, in silent greeting, carried in the symbol of the peacock.

On my birthday in 1996, I had a dream in which:

> *I find a peacock in a yard, while all around busy traffic, work, etc., is going on. It is stunningly beautiful with iridescent colours. His tail is not in display—maybe not quite old enough. He is very friendly to me and comes up into my arms. I hold him. I am worried about traffic and want to hide him but am told not to worry. There is a mate in the yard too. This dream gave me a feeling of something emerging in its own time, something very beautiful.*

I shared the dream with my mentor who sent an e-mail back to me:

> *Dear John . . . very important the peacock comes to you . . . you are a friendly holder in the busy-ness of the world. Who has time for peacocks?! If one thinks of this as a task (as well as a privilege) then it IS your task to hold the peacock until it's ready. It's not necessarily something you've done yet, perhaps something still to come. Clearly though this is a promising dream. (An interesting word - promise = 'to let go, send forth'). So, I think the unconscious is promising you something, it has sent forth to you the peacock, for you to hold it. Don't necessarily think of it as something already experienced, i.e., keep your eyes open to see what you find in the "busyness" of the world. And what of the mate? A generative image and further promise!*

Lastly, he added:

> *Do look to the sky later this month and see the brightest comet in four hundred years, Comet Hyakutake, last around here about 10,000 years ago!*

This birthday in 1996 was particularly important to me in other ways too. The previous six years had been a time of tremendous hardship for me. My astrological chart had been ruled by transiting Saturn which was sitting squarely on my Sun-Jupiter in *Aquarius*, my sun sign. It was in this period that I was faced with the reality of everything Saturn stood for—the weight of time, responsibility, discipline, money worries, the impossibility of outer movement, constriction, depression. But by 1996 Saturn had moved across to Pisces and Uranus had moved into *Aquarius*. Uranus is of course the ruler of *Aquarius* where it is exalted, as they say. The timing of this new astrological configuration, with my dream and its hint of a promise of things to come, felt "right" in the sense of a meaningful coincidence.

On a cloudy afternoon of March 24, L. and I set off to view the comet *Hyakutake*, heading east over the mountains to find a possible location to view the comet peeking through the thick cloud cover that is so much a part of the Northwest weather. It didn't look promising. We drove for about two hours into Eastern Washington, left the freeway, and began meandering along the country roads of Wenatchee. We were following our noses, and each other's suggestions: down this way, across this beautiful river, around a bend, tracing the contours of a low hill. The hill looked promising as a viewing spot but the clouds were still thick as the day drew to a close. We didn't know what we looking for yet the way in which we went back and forth helping each other along the way suggested strongly to me later, when I reflected on the whole episode, that we were being purposeful in the sense of *telos*—having purpose yet the goal remaining hidden or unknown.

At last we turned the final corner and stopped the car. We had indeed arrived at the place where we needed to be, yet neither of us had known of its existence. There before us were peacocks. It would have been startling enough to see one peacock but there were several trees filled with them. We were at a peacock farm. Apparently they were retiring for the night. Several crossed the road in front of us as we sat in silence, marvelling. There was no need to go any further so we got out and watched for some time as these wondrous birds, bedecked in their fine iridescent plumage moved around us, quite unafraid. Like the peacock in my dream, they were not in season as their tail feathers were not full grown. L. and I beheld this display in quiet wonder, both very moved, until it became dark. Then, in yet another spontaneous gesture of mutual accord, we turned the car up a little dirt track that revealed itself and led us up the hill where the peacocks were also heading.

There, among the tall firs that crowned over us, we found a dry patch, spread a blanket, and waited in the cooling night. We even napped a little. I lay on my back looking up in the direction of the Big Dipper, which I could just see peeking through the clouds. I watched for a couple of hours and witnessed what modern people see so very seldom—the great vault of heaven moving over me, silent and vast. The Big Dipper arced its way westward degree by degree and about 11pm, a window opened up in the clouds revealing the full glory of the night sky. There was the Big Dipper unveiled now and near its handle, a soft ball of white light with a tail spreading outwards from it across half the sky above us. We were granted a clear view of the Comet *Hyakutake*, the comet that had last been seen 10,000 years ago.

It is such a peculiar feeling to witness in silent stillness such a grand spectacle of light that seems so full of motion and sound. The comet did not move relative to us except as the Sphere of Heaven arced overhead, slowly and majestically. The great tail of the comet which suggested so many "whooshing" sounds remained poised in suspension. The effect was to produce a moment which felt so portentous, pregnant with meaning. Comets have always been seen this way, i.e., as portends of the future and now I was feeling it, personally. 10,000 years is a long time between visits and I marvelled at the fact that 10,000 years is the time span that Joseph Campbell uses to measure the emergence and final decline of the great City States, ruled by the Priest-Kings. In this long span of time, the foundational myth was of the universe as an orderly mandala in which every aspect of earthly existence has its allotted place and role to be fulfilled in concert with the whole—just as the planets do, revolving faithfully in their orbits, forever regular.

I had the privilege to witness the second appearance of the comet that had ushered in a cultural era lasting 10,000 years and which may be presiding over the death of this same era, now at the end of this millennium.

After a while the clouds closed over again, as if to draw the curtain finally, on this extraordinary day, and perhaps, era.

I dream of a peacock, holding the promise of something to come; peacocks appear as harbingers in my outer life; a comet appears and associations are made between my own transformation, peacocks, and comets. At the same time I learn that comets, peacocks, and transformation are connected on the macrocosmic scale as well. Comets have long been associated with portentous events in history, particularly violent catastrophe, and the tail of the comet is likened to that of the peacock, as indeed is the entire sky. Both are also connected with the crow (see my essay, *Augury of the Crow*): [7]

> *The serene and starry sky and the shining sun are peacocks. The deep-blue firmament shining with a thousand brilliant eyes, and the sun rich with the colours of the rainbow, present the appearance of a peacock in all the splendour of its eye-bespangled feathers. When the sky or the thousand-rayed sun . . . is hidden by clouds, or veiled by autumnal mists, it again resembles the peacock, which, in the dark part of the year, like a great number of vividly coloured birds, sheds its beautiful plumage, and becomes drab and unadorned; the crow which had*

---

[7]   (Jung, 1976)

put on the peacock's feathers then caws with the other
crows in funereal concert. In winter the peacock-crow
has nothing left to it except its shrill disagreeable cry,
which is not dissimilar to that of the crow.

(De Gubernatis, quoted in Jung, par. 291

The next five years were filled with terror-driven storms during which I was initiated into those soul qualities that form a lighthouse (see my essay, *Lighthouse at the End of the World*). Meanwhile my dream of promise in which I hold the peacock with his mate nearby was quietly being fulfilled—the dragon of desire and fear transforming into a peacock. Two realities colliding within me—fire and water. From their violent union springs a thing of beauty and love.

Shortly after the evening of the comet, a poem came to me:

peacock

threads twining
peacock tail forming
pollen path golden lustrous
spider web silvered droplets
reflect in each golden mane
of the magnificent one
captured in sparkling diamonds
tawny yellowed sun
his glory
kisses smooth skins
sending his power
in rainbows
pulsing forth to a world
so desperately in need of
his satiny touch

FROM DREAM TO WORLD

Your life is a High Gothic novel!

The dream announcement startled me. There were no "visual" images in the dream. It was simply a voice making a simple statement. I had received a metaphor in which two normally unrelated facts—my life and High Gothic novels—were spontaneously connected in an identity that up till now had escaped me.

The dream was so compact in form and unfamiliar that I felt stupid. With many dreams, at least the dreamer gets enough familiar images (of family, work, friends, etc.) that he or she can commit the usual folly of dismissing the dream as *known*. Not so in this case. But the dream did begin to nudge me. My memory began to stir in response to the dream and associations unintended by me gathered around like a silent crowd of people coming into a room, not knowing quite what to do with one another, but expectant, waiting for something to happen.

My first visitor was a memory of Walter Benjamin's approach to metaphor. I quickly looked up a quote I had written some time ago, not knowing at the time why it grabbed me so.

Whereas my life is intertwined with the history of the second half of this century (I was born in 1950), Benjamin belonged to the first half. He was influenced in the most original and peculiar ways by artistic, social and political movements in Germany and Europe, where he lived and worked. Like a true heuristic researcher he was only interested in those perspectives and the concepts they used to the extent that they could usefully contribute to an exploration of his own fascinations: [8]

> *What fascinated him about the matter (of Marxist thought) was that the spirit and its material manifestation were so intimately connected . . . He was concerned with the correlation between a street scene, a speculation on the stock exchange, a poem, a thought, with the hidden line which holds them together and enables the historian or philologist to recognize that they must all be placed in the same period . . .*
>
> *In his concern with directly, actually demonstrable concrete facts, with single events and occurrences whose "significance" is manifest, Benjamin was not much interested in theories or "ideas" which did not immediately assume the most precise outward shape imaginable. To this very complex but still highly realistic mode of thought the Marxian relationship between superstructure and substructure became, in a precise sense, a metaphorical one . . . provided that "metaphor" is understood in its original, nonallegorical sense of metapherein (to transfer). For a metaphor establishes a connection which is sensually perceived in its immediacy and requires no interpretation . . .*
>
> *Since Homer the metaphor has borne that element of the poetic which conveys cognition; its use establishes the* correspondences *between physically most remote things . . . Metaphors are the means by which the oneness of the world is poetically brought about.* (11-14)

My life in a secret identity with a High Gothic novel, giving material form to the invisible! If a metaphor "establishes a connection which is sensually perceived in its immediacy and requires no interpretation," then my dream suggests the possibility of others reading my life as one would a book, a piece of literature.

---

[8]   (Benjamin, 1968)

Or a book may be writing itself through the vicissitudes of my life. If my dream were more than idiosyncratic, it suggests in general that the psyche is intending that a connection between history and literature be made conscious—in the life of an individual!

This was a momentous idea for me, and still deeply unconscious. As I often do when faced with my own unconsciousness, I began searching around amongst the available pool of ideas for some sort of corroboration even if the learning remains "on the outside".

I read Hillman's discussion of the connection between soul and history in which I found a startling similarity to what my dream was saying: [9]

> For us, it would mean remembering first our individual soul history, its heroic encounters and its pilgrimage, its history as an epic process, a Canterbury tale, eternally valid, historical but timeless. Jung's own biography, which places his outer history within the mythos of his psyche, is an important contemporary example. Even in this realm of history and biography, Jung re-found the old way and brought it back to life. (8)

At this point my mind became excited and wanted to take off with this idea and study it as an emergent theme in the worlds of literature and psychology, e.g., a study of biography. But such an approach to the dream material, i.e., studying it as conscious content would lead me away from the unconscious intent of the dream. If I were to align with the intent of the dream then I had to rein in those horses of the intellect and continue to follow the hints that emerged *spontaneously* in me, in response to the dream itself.

What was my psyche next drawn to? I became curious about the word "gothic". Like many others I used the word casually to denote certain cathedrals in Europe but the meaning of the word remained in the dark for me. I began to gather some readings.

---

[9]   (Hillman, 1979)

I found out that Gothic architecture was governed by logical formalism, scholasticism, etc., of the Middle Ages for 400 years in Europe.

The word was revived in the 19th century to name those novels dealing with horror and the supernatural, e.g., Frankenstein and Dracula. Digging deeper into the history of the word I found that it is a name for the Germans, i.e., the Visigoths, one of the tribes of Europe who sacked the Roman Empire. I became intrigued about how the name for the tribe could have become attached to Middle Age architecture and later, a certain kind of novel.

So, I looked up Grolier's Encyclopaedia (1996) and learned that Gothic novels expressed an imagination of the 18th century in which was conjured up: [10]

> . . . a medieval world of barbarous passions enacted in picturesque melodramatic settings of ruined castles, ancient monasteries, and wild landscapes. Within a plot designed for suspense, a delicate feminine sensibility is subjected to the onslaught of elemental forces of good and evil. Sanity and chastity are constantly threatened, and over all looms the suggestion that evil and irrationality will destroy civilization.

The Goth as pillagers of Rome, marking the decline of an ancient world as defined by Renaissance writers probably formed the historical background to this literary expression of 18th century soul life.

In the middle of this research, a personal memory bubbled up—one which was embarrassing. When I was a teenager at school I foolishly told my friends of a powerful fantasy of saving a young frightened girl from a burning school building—she jumps into my arms. I was of course ridiculed but now 32 years later I can see the traces of a Gothic imagination running through me

---

[10]   (Batchelor, 1996)

in the image of rescuing the young delicate soul from a collapsing civilization.

Up to now my research had the phenomenology of "looking upon" facts that remained outside of me. But when that particular personal memory surfaced, apparently in response to my research, I *felt* a connection between my dream, the historical facts and my own interiority. With that memory I got a sense of how my life *could* be a High Gothic novel and how it might be experienced by others that way, even if the result at times is ridicule.

To bring the intent of the dream into consciousness, the major clue that I had so far uncovered lay in the relationship between soul and history. I found how my life could be a High Gothic novel only when I remembered a moment from my own history. This memory is apparently of interest to my soul since it emerged spontaneously.

I could easily remember other events of my school life which have become part of my "official record". These kinds of conscious memory (my school grades, who I hated at school, my first car, etc.,) are repeated to myself and others when asked about my adolescent years. They carry the phenomenology of the mundane—there are no surprises or anomalies. Instead there is regularity, repetition, routine, and appearance of continuity. These memories together are a narrative with no plot: "I did this then this happened then this, etc." In psychological terms they form the content of my modern ego which is an organ that likes to view its past as a completely known continuous line of events. Gaps in that life are treated as pathologies (amnesia, dissociative disorder, trauma etc).

My spontaneous memory was not part of that official record and instead it carried qualities of surprise, discontinuity, suddenness, and anomaly. But it still was my history and it was only with *this* kind of memory that I found a meaningful link between my personal history and the literary form of the High Gothic novel.

My research so far had released an experience in which I felt a connection between my own life and the period of collective history known as High Gothic with its characteristic form of literature. This aspect of the past lives on in me; in my soul, as it were, and informs the way my own life unfolds. This discovery was very exciting for it opened me up to a deeper question of the relationship between the unfolding of my personal life *and* the historical time into which I was born and live.

Perhaps if I could expand my research into this question with the same methodology, I might find an answer to a problem that seems to be assuming central place as we approach the end of the millennium: namely, the accelerating split between the life of an individual on a local scale and the historical events that surround that individual on the global scale.

Richard Tarnas describes our modern existential condition this way: [11]

> *We have the post-Copernican dilemma of being a peripheral and insignificant inhabitant of a vast cosmos, and the post-Cartesian dilemma of being a conscious, purposeful, and personal subject confronting an unconscious, purposeless, and impersonal universe.* (420)

When we are so personally disconnected from the universe in this way, life assumes a terrifying scale and magnitude and fear governs our actions which become chaotic. I wondered what kind of actual experience would convince modern individuals that the living of their concrete personal lives could be in a meaningful relationship with world events on the global scale when that global scale seems so "unconscious, purposeless, and impersonal".

I decided to find out in terms of my own life.

I began my research by starting with my own birth year, 1950. I consulted an Almanac to find out what was going on at that time, allowing my psyche to lead the way. That is, I did

---

[11]   (Tarnas, 1991)

not attempt to be exhaustive in my research. Rather, I followed psychic hints which appear as erotic impulses signalling hidden connections between me and the material I was studying.

Here is what I found:

- *The Korean War… President Truman… Truman-McArthur conflict: to contain the war or go on offensive, but there was a Sino-Soviet treaty that threatened Europe and the US and could lead to another World War. A stand-off ensued, leading to Cold War.*
- *McCarthy and anti-Communists rose in power. Their focus was on artists, ruining many careers.*
- *China invaded Tibet.*
- *Mother Teresa founded the Missionaries of Charity.*
- *Tacoma Narrows Bridge was built, one of the longest suspension bridges in US.*
- *Suzuki began his lifelong travel.*
- *The US established the Subversive Activities Control Board. Subversion was defined as plan or action to overthrow the government, yet it conflicts with freedom of speech. Treason, espionage and sabotage threaten the established order, but how to manage this in a free system.*
- *Wallace Stevens wrote the Auroras of Autumn.*
- *Tape recorder and Xerox were invented.*
- *Jan Oort, Astronomer, made his discovery of the origin of comets beyond our solar system?*
- *Pope Pius XXII announced the Assumption of Mary—* Assumptio Mariae.
- Worlds in Collision *was written by Russian-American physician Immanuel Velikovsky, 55, and draws on mythology, archaeology, astronomy, and other disciplines to evolve a theory that the Earth barely avoided colliding with several other celestial bodies sometime about 3,200 BC.*
- *Truman gave the go ahead for the development of the hydrogen bomb.*

As I chronicled these events throughout the world in 1950, I felt a thread of excitement gathering around the spontaneously forming association that linked certain of these events: the Cold War, the pope, the *Assumptio Mariae*, and the end of the world (comets, worlds in collision, invasion of Tibet).

The methodology of my research demands that I remain available to whatever stirs in my psyche in response to my engagement with this history of the outer world at the time of my birth. So, as I was recording these events, a childhood memory suddenly emerged: *From Russia, with Love*—James Bond! I loved to read his exploits, especially that book which tells the story of his passionate and dangerous affair with the lovely Russian spy and how their love won through in spite of the Cold War placing them as implacable enemies. I saw the movie several times.

I then remembered two other personal connections to Russia. I was in love with Natalie Woods, the actress who played in *West Side Story*. Of course, she was Russian—Natasha—and when I was still at college I met V. and fell deeply in love. V. was Russian as well.

These were isolated experiences that had imprinted themselves deeply in my soul, but any meaning that might link them in some way had remained quite in the dark. It was only as I began my research that a hint came. There is some connection between my soul life, Russia, and love.

This connection deepened considerably as I began to remember a sequence of many dreams I had over the years during my own spiritual ordeal. [12] When I was 29 years old, I had arrived in Los Angeles and somehow found my way into Jungian analysis where the floodgates opened and I was inundated with dream material that scoured out new riverbeds into which my life subsequently flowed. The primary symbol that emerged at that time was the serpent whose appearance pointed to a fate appearing in my life. This feeling has not gone away since that time, and indeed has

---

[12]   See my other books published also with *iUniverse*.

intensified as I turned more of my attention to the many dreams and sequences that flowed out over the years.

Several particular dream sequences had occurred, of Russia, the pope, the goddess, and materialism. Though I wrote the dreams down and explored their implications, I had not found any connection between them at the time. I had never even considered them simultaneously at all.

In my dreams of Russia over the years, I had found myself "in Siberia", speaking or understanding the Russian language or somehow being involved in the political realities in Russia. I also had a long sequence of dreams in which I experienced quite intimate relations with the bear, which of course is the symbol of Russia. One "Russian" dream was particularly impactful:

> *I am underground in a tunnel, a subway. A small cart comes along the tracks with gifts, one for me, with my name on it. A juggernaut, a subway train, comes and pushes the cart back into the tunnel where I can't reach it. I follow it to get my parcel. I arrive at a terminal and a man shows me the wrappings of the gift. The gift is gone. I feel bereft, isolated, impoverished, typical feelings of my childhood. Then a scene opens up on the world stage. Gorbachev and Yeltsin are working on a plan. Yeltsin says, "Well, let's come back later and do some more". Gorbachev looks at him very tenderly and embraces him with real warmth, between two former advisors. It was a moment of genuine love between them.*

My early attempts to release meaning from this and other dreams was typical of the kind of psychological "parochialism" that pervades the discipline today. "Siberia" of course was "my" wasteland; my "understanding Russian" after emerging from an altered state (within the dream) was reduced to my coming out of a private world and rejoining the local community. "Yeltsin" and "Gorbachev" embracing on the world stage was a reflection of two halves of my own masculinity joining up. I also noted that Gorbachev is *Piscean* and Yeltsin is *Aquarian*, so that the dream could have to do with the transition from the *Piscean* age to the *Aquarian* age. The bears were my own chthonic nature embracing me, etc. And so, with these reductive interpretations, ego consciousness increased around chthonic masculinity, relationship to the collective, my fear of alienation and so on. All these interpretations quite ignored the precision of the images which seemed to be quite definitely going on about *Russia* and my soul's participation in her history.

Over the same period of time I had dreams concerning the Pope. It is easy enough now to discern a psychological inflation in some of them but as that problem began to soften, the dreams kept coming. Something kept putting me in relationship to the Pope:

> *I am sitting with the Pope and the American archbishop. I am talking animatedly with the Bishop about materialism reaching its end. "It's taken its time," he said. I agreed and said that it must be lived through to the end before something else can emerge. I was charged with a fire that suffused my face which glowed. The Bishop got caught up in our discussion, interrupting me but the Pope saw that I was infused with spirit and leaned over to his Bishop saying in a soft voice, in Latin, to listen, stay quiet, don't stop him from talking, that I somehow understood . . . we sat in the silence. He watched me carefully, my face glowing softly, then his eyes rolled back and he said some more in Latin that I could not catch.*

This dream shows a link between me the Pope, and the problem of materialism, but there is still another sequence of dreams I had concerning the goddess—dreams that showed a kind of intimacy between myself and the goddess of the world. She had often appeared to me in her wrathful destructive form, enraged over the treatment she has received at the hands of men. Yet inexplicably, within that rage which seemed beyond propitiation, she revealed to me the incredible depth of her suffering, and indeed the cure of that suffering. To compound the mystery, several times in these dreams, she freely granted me a gift. In one such dream (1985):

> In the forest I see some people spurn Grandmother, the goddess whom I love and revere. I become frightened as I know she will return in her terrible aspect. E. and I leave the forest. In a house, I hear her coming, chanting, "MIA DUBBO DOLMO!" In the next room I hear a man screaming endlessly, shrieking in terror and agony as he burns up. Now our door opens and I know she is coming towards me. I place E. behind me, stand up, eyes on the floor, arms stretched out towards her and call out, "Grandmother, this is your son. I love you and remember you. I know these people have insulted you. I have not! I love and honour you!" I see on the floor a deep fiery red appear with a burning acrid smell. I dare not look up. She hears my prayer. The flames retreat. She goes to continue her path of revenge. I vow to place a cairn at the place she was spurned.

Although each of these sequences of dreams of Russia, the pope, and the goddess opened me to many areas of personal unconsciousness, none of them could be reduced in entirety to unconsciousness of my personal self unless "Russia", "the pope", "the goddess", and "materialism" were theoretically taken as projections, having nothing to do with those actualities. This theoretical position is of course dominant in psychology today. The basis of this theory lies in Cartesian philosophy in which self and world are fundamentally separate and nothing of the world can appear in the self. From this world view, dreams are taken as images of the personal self and so an image of "Russia" for example is understood as an image of me, having nothing to do with the actual country. Maybe it is that aspect of myself that is totally foreign to me, at war with itself, splitting up, walled off from the rest of me, "the pope" is my grandiosity, or the aspect that speaks *ex-cathedra*, or my traditional religious side, but not having anything to do with the real pope, whom I have never met. His image in my dream is but an image of me, projected onto the real pope, according to this world view of self and other.

To be sure, I examined all these dreams from this theoretical position and indeed discovered elements of my personal shadow but was left unsatisfied with the feeling that in some way I had not yet served the felt intentionality in these dreams. Yet for many years I could do nothing more until several unusual happenings effectively destroyed my identification with the Cartesian position. I was effectively initiated into another reality and thus could consider my dreams of Russia, the pope, and the goddess from within a new perspective governed by a principle, not of disjunction but of interpenetration.

The first unusual happening occurred when, acting on an impulse I went to the Internet and typed in "Russia", such a move being true to my methodology in which I was to follow the hints from psyche in response to the research I was doing. Quite a few web sites came up of course, which led to others until I landed at the Vatican web site. A hyperlink (1997) led in turn to one called simply "Fatima" which I had never heard of before. I read: [13]

> *Fatima is a town in Portugal and:*
>
> *The Blessed Virgin Mary, the Mother of God, appeared six times to three shepherd children ("the Three Seers") near the town of Fatima, Portugal between May 13 and October 13, 1917. Appearing to the children, the Blessed Virgin told them that She had been sent by God with a message for every man, woman and child living in our century.*
>
> *Coming at a time when civilization was torn asunder by war and bloody violence, She promised that Heaven would grant peace to all the world if Her requests for prayer,*

---

[13]   www.fatima.org which has been substantially revised (2012) since the time of writing this essay (1995)

reparation and consecration were heard and obeyed. "If My
requests are granted . . . there will be peace."

. . . God's Mother prophesied that Russia would be God's
chosen "instrument of chastisement," spreading the "errors" of
atheism and materialism across the earth, fomenting wars,
annihilating nations and persecuting the Faithful everywhere.
"If My requests are not granted, Russia will spread its errors
throughout the world, raising up wars and persecutions against
the Church. The good will be martyred, the Holy Father will
suffer much and various nations will be annihilated."

. . . The second part of the Secret specifically prophesized the
outbreak of World War II and contained the Mother of God's
solemn request for the Consecration of Russia as a condition of
world peace. It also predicted the inevitable triumph of Her
Immaculate Heart following Russia's consecration and the
conversion "of that poor nation" to the Catholic Faith.

Here in a few short paragraphs, the sequences of dreams I
had concerning the Pope, Russia, the goddess, and materialism
were woven together into the fabric of an actual historical event,
and a prophesy of the end of the world!

I was profoundly shaken by this powerful moment of
discovery. I felt the experience of the end of one world and the
opening up of another, as an apocalypse occurring within my
own psyche. The Cartesian world into which we are each born
today was ending in me. The world in which the opposites are
sundered, particularly the inner subjective one and the outer
objective one, was collapsing. A new world in which "inner"
and "outer" were interpenetrating in a very mysterious way was
coming to birth in me.

I was particularly gripped by the image of the consecration
of Russia to the heart of the goddess. This apparently was
necessary to avoid catastrophe and achieve world peace. The act
of consecration in the Catholic Church means to bring into the
fold of church through an act of love. This would constitute a
powerful gesture in which Russia and the rest of the world would

be united. The terrible opposition would be overcome through an act of love that says in effect: this "poor nation" too belongs to our wholeness.

The various popes accepted that the visions of Fatima were genuine, i.e., of the goddess Mary, yet successive popes consistently refused do her exact bidding. Apparently her command conflicted with the political interests going on between the Russian Orthodox Church, the Vatican and the Soviet Government. Power won over love and Russia has never been fully consecrated. I was disturbed and shocked by this news yet felt how typical! We want to be saved as long as the saving grace does not interfere with our immediate parochial interests. This episode is a colossal example of free will choosing security over the unusual and unexpected. I have been guilty of this many times in my own local scale.

The next unusual happening occurred soon after. If I had any doubts at all about the intentionality of the psyche in connecting my soul life to Russia, love and the goddess, they were swept away completely in a particular *moment*. My initiation into the world in which spirit and matter interpenetrate, in which matter becomes an expression *of* spirit was deepened considerably.

It began in an ordinary way. I was invited to an evening of dream sharing hosted by my friend R. I had no plan. I did decide to bring along some clay pieces I had recently made following another intense encounter with kundalini energies. [14] I drove into the car park just as another car pulled in. A beautiful young woman emerged who asked me how to get to the basement where the meeting was being held. I simply said, "Go down!"—smart ass! In the room afterwards, I met her again and chatted. Actually I was doom-saying about the future of therapy, my favourite gripe at the time. My friend approached us and asked if we came together. I said no but again wise-cracked that it was love at first sight.

---

[14]　See my book *Making of a Man: Initiation Through the Divine Mother*, published by iUniverse.

No one seemed to know her. I began to feel that maybe it wasn't just a wise-crack and I decided to sit next to her and so the evening began. People shared this or that until a coffee break. When we came back I felt one of my urges to speak. I could feel what I was going to say and the images flowed. I began to speak about my path, how I was convinced of the connection between my personal hardships and the suffering in the world. I spoke about my need to give form to that connection. I described my attempts so far. I mentioned my dreams of the pope, Mary and Russia, leading to Fatima, and the link to my birth year and the historical record at that time. I further spoke of recent dreams showing my active participation in healing the conflict in Russia and asked how could this be? Yet if I believed my dreams I would have to dispense with ideas of a separate self, etc., and to follow instead ideas such as interpenetration. I spoke of how this and other ideas had led me out of therapy as a viable cultural form. I had to find another way to live my convictions.

I was really into it by now, particularly about the mystery drawing me to the suffering of Russia. Then, I was done.

I believe many there felt a palpable presence (I checked later) in what happened next. The young woman, A., with whom I had spoken just a few words, and who was now sitting right next to me said that it was her turn now because she comes from Russia! My heart stopped. She introduced herself to everybody by singing us a song in Russian in honour of her father who followed his dreams. I began to shake like a leaf. She turned to me and said, "The boundaries are dissolving—watch out!"

Threads weaving together: Russia, love, the pope and the goddess! And, like a mosaic slowly coming into form, a young woman who embodies this complex tapestry emerges into focus.

What possible response from me could be adequate to the magnitude of what I felt? All at once I felt two worlds collide in me. The historical events that linked the church with Russia, love and the goddess had suddenly materialized in an encounter between souls. I was personally experiencing an historical event on the local scale.

What can come of such a collision of realities—an objective historical reality interpenetrating with a personal soul reality? If, as the goddess at Fatima says, the organ that can contain such opposites is the heart, then perhaps what comes out this collision is a new reality based on *interpenetration*—a reality that needs its own language.

And so, the only response I had left came from my heart in yet another stream of spontaneous poetry (poesis). Several poems were thus born from our encounter:

wassilisa the beautiful

circle broken, innocence lost
from the cave of the dark mother
now called forth.
beautiful wassilisa enters
the dark forest of the mother

afraid, yet curious
picking her way cautiously
through the thick bushes
a clearing

pausing, listening …

bursting through huge oaks
three knights
charging the air with power
dust billowing senses filling
sexual steam of man, stallion and dark earth

whirling about
mad intoxicating power of an army
graceful precision of dancing masters
white red and black warriors
creaking leather

din and clashing
shields on cover'd thighs
threatening teasing
power to kill at a stroke
power to caress into joy.

surrounded by metalled whirling dervishes
no escape from war trained hooves
sharpened to kill on command
dancing in and out
slightest nudge from expert knee
visor'd hidden face of his master
closer closer to her trembling form
springing away
gazelle fleeing lion.
standing still at the centre
seeing her own gray-blue eyes
flashing off every silver'd curve
of horse and rider
those eyes she sees are not afraid
wonder and excitement
wide and alive
drinking in saturated scene
of wild masculinity.
trembling in her body
no not fear
something else …

longing for that darkness
that deep deep darkness
that alone yields up such chthonic powers

who are you?
bursting forth from her throat

amused silence greets her
quiet stillness settling
soft thunderous breath
tossing heads flicking tails.
flaring nostrils,
black eyes ears alert

all focus to the centre
where she stands
poised
*   . . . deep silence tightening*
*   stringing harp*

never has she felt so alive
as in that silence!
deep from within her own being
whispering
rising into torrent
roaring rapids
somehow somehow she knows!
she will not be harmed
rising up from depths of her own being
joyous cry
passionate revelation

answering cry
exultant praise
shouting forth from the three.
lances rising abruptly vertical salute
heels slapping hard
steaming flanks
reins pulling
sharp urgent turn
leaves dust scattering
knights steeds quickly folding
green brown glooming forest

rolling thunder
distant retreating hills
wassilisa the beautiful
hair mingling with dust musky trails
watching those departing ones

starting in her womb
dark glowing coal
hint of smoldering redness
in clear gray eyes
something now ignited
she must now know more.

no longer young girl
tentatively picking way into woods
frightened at every snap of twig or scurrying animal
wassilisa
striding forward down
thorns tearing dress opening skin
down down down to the centre

baba yaga calling for her
now wassilisa seeking!

she knows, she knows
answering her own question

who are you?

she sees, she sees
dark silver trail on forest floor
link to dark mother
womb to womb

no longer clear
who is calling whom
they will meet
they must meet
transmission of wisdom
must take place
chthonic wisdom
mistress of wild beasts
wisdom
so few are willing
to be near.

baba yaga now found her servant
servant now has
found herself.

mermaid

crowd gathers
centering young woman
struggling to walk
tune of derision mockery
only a cane to help her
legs so long and slender
curving stretching down
feet ending
strangely bending toes

no one knows her
where does she come from?
dark hair damply hanging
long shoulder sloping

brave souls addressing
song breathing from her lips
brave souls retreating

crowd offers more distant observations

such strange musical notes
escaping her mouth

moved to silence at first
distant memory stirring
bells water
tinkling against stone
tones
uncanny echoes blue depths
long forgotten by mankind.

but among men
this beautiful silence of possibilities
so quickly filling
with known safety of fear

rock found
passing hand to hand
air suddenly cracking tight
rope pulled hard.

i am pulled too
but towards her
in that moment i see

eyes blue-gray reflections
sky upon water
hair windswept waves
legs strong lean
awkward hurting
toes not deformed at all
transparent skin webs
more used to a friendlier touch
than what hard ground can offer

voice echoing another world
we once knew
now left far behind

love welling in my heart
music filling
penetrating
awakening dormant knowing
gentle tinkling sea bells,
deep moans of leviathan
forming words within me

emerging from deep immersion in her
seeing rock raised to throw
stepping forward
crowd giving way
wave parting

stop! can't you see?
she is not crippled
she is a mermaid a mermaid a mermaid
she is not seeking alms or favours
she is seeking . . . us
listen to her
listen
i have come! i have come! i have come!
greetings! i have come!

MEANING OF THE BOMB
AS WORLD DESTROYER

Introduction

"There are three powers that belong together," my friend said to me, "*love, wisdom,* and *might*! We have such a poor relationship to might today as may be seen in the current weather patterns and natural disasters".

What an extraordinary statement to hear! He was telling me that there is a connection between our relationship to *might* and the natural weather patterns and events in the world. There is nothing in our current world view, dominated as it by science, which would support such a claim. Only a physical causal connection could be seen from that world view and of course such a claim as my friend's would be nonsense.

Yet some hint of another kind of connection surely emerges in the words that burst forth from Oppenheimer's lips when the first atomic explosion was witnessed by the scientists at Los Alamos. The story of Oppenheimer's moments during the first atomic explosion is recalled by Rose in his *Integrity Papers:* [15]

> *Two fascinating stories about Robert Oppenheimer, considered the innovator behind the creation of the A-Bomb, show us just what perceptions and language and ideas are all about. His vision of phenomena was remarkable. When asked some years after viewing the first atomic bomb explosion, he recalled that as he "saw" the billowing glowing atomic cloud of radiation*

---

[15] Rose, James H. (2000). *Integrity Papers*. www.ceptualinstitute.com (no longer available)

he was in fact seeing the second and third derivatives
(factors of mathematical Calculus equations) vanish
infinitesimally. *His physical eyes were looking at*
one reality while his mind was appreciating another
perception just as conceptually real . . .

In that terrible moment when the bomb came into being, Oppenheimer had a dual "perception". His ordinary perception of a "billowing glowing atomic cloud of radiation" belongs to the world of science, one which is the dominant form of consciousness in the world today. This form of consciousness is commonly known as "Cartesian". It is a self-consciousness "in here" which is set against a world of matter "out there" without consciousness, a world of matter that can therefore be studied and manipulated as a thing. This was no doubt Oppenheimer's customary form of consciousness. But in that same moment, he also had a very different "perception" of the world: "second and third derivatives (factors of mathematical Calculus equations) vanish infinitesimally . . ." From this second "perception" apparently burst a poetic expression of the spirit in its destructive aspect from Oppenheimer's lips in the form of a quote from Hindu scripture, "I am Death, destroyer of worlds!"

For the purposes of this essay it does not matter if this quote is apocryphal. The phenomenology is consistent with the experience of many pioneer scientists who make original contributions, the *joy* of which is expressed as lying in the discovery of a felt connection between an inner psychic state (flow of equations, dream, image, etc.,) and the exterior world.

Oppenheimer's first perception is born of Cartesian consciousness which looks *upon* the world of dead matter, with no participation in that world. His second "perception" (really a *thinking*) is born from another kind of consciousness altogether, one that is participatory. He was no longer looking upon the surface of things but instead "perceived" the *interiority* of things, their soul. He experienced, for a moment, the world as an expression of spirit and thus the atomic bomb was seen for what it really is—the material manifestation of a spiritual reality in the world.

When the material world is actually perceived as an expression of spiritual reality, then we can begin to understand statements such as my friend's. The eruption of the atomic bomb into material reality and the ensuing Cold War with its escalation into a nuclear nightmare shows without doubt our "poor relationship" to *might*. In other words, the *might* or power that we see outside ourselves as a quality of a material outer event or thing may be experienced as an image of a spiritual reality "within". Oppenheimer had such an unexpected experience momentarily, under conditions of great emotion and it seems that the effects continued for the rest of his life.

Nonetheless, our "poor relationship" to *might* continues unabated, finding even more frightening and subtle forms in the world with our increasing penetration into the atomic realm with genetics and with the high tech industry, for example. Our pursuit of knowledge for the sole purpose of manipulating nature is accelerating with consequences that are even less predictable than those of the atomic bomb in 1945.

These considerations have led me to ask if there is an actual path by which a human being can come into a "right relationship" with this awesome spiritual aspect of *might*. If Oppenheimer can offer us any clue about this path it would be this: we would find a way of moving from a world of exteriority, with the corresponding experience of ourselves as "inner" and thus divided from that world, *to* a realization of the world as an expression *of* spiritual reality with the corollary of an actual participation in that world.

If there is such a path, it would clearly be one of initiation.

WAY OF THE DREAM

Owen Barfield wrote a remarkable little book in which he describes a dialogue with a voice that carries tremendous wisdom.[16] The voice identifies itself as a messenger of Michael, an angelic power that seeks to aid human beings in the next stage of the evolution of consciousness. One of the most compelling and difficult instructions that Barfield (as the character Burgeon in the book) faces concerns the mystery of nature and transformation. *The Meggid* tells Burgeon:

> *That which is the might of the spirit within you, when it is encountered from without, as it must be if you are to be freed of its compulsion is—nature. Will you choose to confront her as enemy or will you seek to welcome and understand her as friend?* (114)

In other words, this angelic being is introducing the proposition that our present reality of separate independent existence paired as it is with the physical world lying wholly outside of us can become, once transformed, a participatory one in which the world becomes an *expression* of a spiritual reality, in this case "the *might* of the spirit within you".
He goes on:

> *Your brothers in the West will learn, indeed they are beginning to suspect already that within each of them, deep hidden and hitherto unconscious, there lives a fury of destructive force, beside which the destructive forces in nature pale.* (158)

Over a long period of time I found own way to the momentous discovery of the *might* which we normally encounter in nature occurring as "might of the spirit within you". I also discovered

---

16   (Barfield, 1965)

exactly how, in my own life, the "time of (man's) shelter is drawing to a close".

For twenty years I endured an ordeal of fire. [17] During the day, for hours, days, and weeks at a time, I was stricken with symptoms of heat running through my body. My symptoms reached an unbearable peak at times, with fiery eruptions in my skin producing peeling every few days. My skin was shedding like a snake. I looked sunburned, but the source of heat was not external. My symptoms were pinpricks of fire, like insects stinging me on my face neck, back. My face swelled from the "bites" until I could hardly see through my swollen eye lids. At times I was driven to despair by the intensity of the symptoms. As the quality of my symptoms shifted according to some mysterious intention, I received dreams that acted as a kind of mentor, inviting me to find the connection between the quality of my symptoms and my soul life. In other words I slowly began to perceive my symptoms, not merely as surface, material facts but as qualities of soul, expressions of a spiritual drama of which I was only a part.

I no longer sought out medical or allopathic help for my condition, even though, as I said, I was brought to the brink of despair many times. In turning away from explanations of my condition in terms of material causes, my path in effect became initiatory. I turned more and more to my dreams as hints of what was happening to me spiritually. I became convinced that I was encountering the "*might* of the spirit" within and that collective categories of experience could no longer help me. I became cut off from the community, alone and facing a kind of power that at times seemed intent only on destroying me, so severe were the effects on me. However, as C.G. Jung says (paraphrasing), when one is oppressed by the spirit, one may turn *to* the spirit to find an advocate. And so my dreams brought me knowledge of what was happening to

---

[17]   (Woodcock, 2009)

me and also brought me hints as to how to proceed in the face
of the overwhelming *might* of the spirit:

> *I witness/participate in a nuclear bomb attack. We see*
> *several bombs explode and the hot waves of radiation*
> *envelop us. So they finally did it. We get into a house for*
> *protection.*
>
> *The bomb! I am to suffer and endure consciously the*
> *effects of the heat and radiation of a thermonuclear bomb. It*
> *goes off near me and I feel the heat roaring through my entire*
> *body. Blood pours out of my mouth and eyes and nose. The*
> *heat is tremendous. It is also extremely sexual.*

I was thus presented in unsparing detail with the symbol that
gave meaning to the symptoms manifesting in me for so many
years of my life: the symbol of the atomic bomb!

DESTRUCTION OF FORM

The atomic bomb burst on the world stage in 1945. From
that time on we have lived with the possibility of wiping out all
life on earth. The secret of the bomb lies in its power to destroy
material form, releasing enormous energy that was bound up in
that form. My dreams and symptoms showed that this material
reality is a collective representation of what resides now within
the human being. If we turn within, we are forced to encounter
this awesome power and face the consequences of the destruction
of material form and the release of energy.

Over a period of years I personally experienced this destruction
of material form in that my outer life disintegrated (career, family,
marriage, finances). In other words, I personally experienced the

destruction of the forms of the world in the sense that Leonard Cohen means: [18]

> [W]e're in a very shabby moment, and neither the literary nor the musical experience really has its finger on the pulse of our crisis. From my point of view, we're in the midst of a Flood, a Flood of biblical proportions. It's both exterior and interior—at this point it's more devastating on the interior level, but it's leaking into the real world. And this flood is of such enormous and biblical proportions that I see everybody holding on in their individual way to an orange crate, to a piece of wood, and we're passing each other in this swollen river that has pretty well taken down all the landmarks, and pretty well overturned everything we've got . . .

My dreams showed that the outer destruction of material form is an expression of what was happening in our collective unconscious being. I was being initiated into a process going on in the soul in this historic moment! We are each living in a time of transformation of collective representations or to put it in common language: the end of the world. Symbols, or images, or structures that bring order and meaning to our lives, containing us as it were in their meaning are being destroyed at an accelerating rate. C.G. Jung endured this collective transformation within his psyche as well, and was able to express its processes eloquently throughout his life: [19]

> I was suddenly seized by an overpowering vision: I saw a monstrous flood covering all the northern and low-lying lands between the North Sea and the Alps. When it came up to Switzerland I saw that the mountains grew

---

[18]   (Iyer, 1998). Article found at http://www.leonardcohenfiles.com/buzz. html (September 22, 2012)

[19]   (Jung, 1989)

higher and higher to protect our country. I realized that a frightful catastrophe was in progress. I saw the mighty yellow waves, the floating rubble of civilization, and the drowned bodies of uncounted thousands. Then the whole sea turned to blood. This vision lasted about one hour. I was perplexed and nauseated, and ashamed of my weakness. (175)

At first, being an experienced psychiatrist, Jung interpreted his visions in terms of a possible psychosis but then:

On August 1 the world war broke out. Now my task was clear: I had to try to understand what had happened and to what extent my own experience coincided with that of mankind in general. Therefore my first obligation was to probe the depths of my own psyche. I made a beginning by writing down fantasies which had come to me during my building game. This work took precedence over everything else. (Ibid, 176)

Jung discovered that he was experiencing the "inside" or soul aspect of what was appearing on the "outside". In my own similar experiences, I learned that the advent of the atomic bomb, as a collective representation of our times, represents the destruction of material form, exposing the ego to "radiation". This is Jung's experience of the same phenomenon:

An incessant stream of fantasies had been released, and I did my best not to lose my head but to find some way to understand these strange things. I stood helpless before an alien world; everything in it seemed difficult and incomprehensible. I was living in a constant state of tension; often I felt as if gigantic blocks of stone were tumbling down upon me. One thunderstorm followed another. My enduring these storms was a question of brute strength. Others have been shattered by them—Nietzsche, and Holderlin, and many others. But there was a demonic strength in me, and from the beginning there was no doubt in my mind that I must find the meaning of what I was experiencing in these fantasies. When I endured these assaults of the unconscious I had an unswerving conviction that I was obeying a higher will, and that feeling continued to uphold me until I had mastered the task. (Ibid, 177)

In my case I was subjected to an incessant stream of "radiation", a process that lasted for years. Jung's incessant stream of fantasies led him to years of work, expressing them in art form (his *Red Book*) and in word pictures (his alchemy, etc.,) and later on in architecture (Bollingen) and stone (his carvings). He understood well enough that he was undergoing a destruction of form, a process that was going on in the world's interior. We could even specify further and say he was undergoing, as I did, the destruction of "the already formed" (*natura naturata*), discovering instead "the forming" powers within (*natura naturans*): [20]

We cannot turn the wheel backwards; we cannot go back to the symbolism that is gone . . . I cannot go back to the Catholic Church, I cannot experience the miracle of the Mass; I know too much about it. I know it is the truth, but it is the truth in a form in which I cannot accept it any more . . . It does not express my psychological condition . . . I need a new form. (par 632)

In my case, I also endured a stream of fantasies and dreams for over twenty years, filling many books. But significantly I also experienced an energetic, radiating stream of what I can only call *living thinking.* I had to carry a notebook around with me at all times so that I could record any spontaneous eruption of strange ego-alien *thinking* that burst in on me. I did indeed heat up, as

[20]   (Jung C. G., 1980)

my dream shows and I had to resort to yogic breathing in order to calm myself in the face of the inner onslaught! Radiation is a *destructive* energetic force, as Barfield was also well aware of (see quote above). As I describe above, for many years I was assailed by this radiation and suffered very painful symptoms in my body.

It seems that, at bottom, the appearance of the atomic bomb on the world stage, as a collective representation, is expressing a process going on our unconscious being that we are all sensing and expressing as the *end of the world!* Its meaning appears to be this:

Our entire system of collective representations, i.e., the already formed (*natura naturata*) is undergoing a death process, releasing the spiritual powers that inform (i.e. *make*) them. This breakdown of form releases tremendous energies, the same energies no doubt that produce worlds in the first place. Any individual that comes close to these energies begins to experience the *fury*, as Barfield says.

But what makes such energies *destructive* to humans? As Jung points put above, many perish. Barfield's book *Unancestral Voice* is an account of his own experience with *living thinking* or *natura naturans*, which he names as a spiritual presence: the *Meggid*. The *Meggid* is not destructive to Barfield. Instead "he" is a wise counselor. Jung too, as time went on experienced a diminution of the *lava flow* and an increase in inner wisdom guiding him, to which he remained faithful throughout his life. I too have experienced this shift in my life.

Wolfgang Giegerich perhaps gives the most satisfactory explanation of the destructive quality in *living thinking*. His book *The Soul's Logical Life* is a carefully argued case for the transformation of the soul taking place in our modern times. [21] He shows convincingly how we have arrived at a time in history where we can discover our own new psychological nature to be what I call *living thinking*. This new soul reality has no referent outside itself. Image is no longer image *of* something else and is

---

[21]   (Giegerich, 2001)

not caused by anything outside itself. Perhaps the most exquisite expression (and description) of this level of soul reality can be found in Dante's *Paradiso*!

The soul reality which Jung discovered is showing us that a momentous transformation is taking place, transforming what it means to be a human being. The informing *living thinking* that we once experienced as "other than ourselves" in the form of gods, wisdom, etc., has disappeared, and left us in a state of absolute meaninglessness. Our former collective representations, once rich in symbolic meaning are destroyed and like Jung, we are bereft.

We look vainly for meaning that we can inhabit, but we have, unbeknown to ourselves, *become* that *living thinking* and our own nature is transformed. No longer is our consciousness Cartesian with its disjunction between subject and object. All "inner-outer" splits are transformed. We can no longer look out on the world as an object that has no relation to ourselves (the mechanical world). Instead we can understand the world as a system of collective representations and further understand that we ourselves have formed that world through the *living thinking* that we now are. Such a transformation of course carries a responsibility with it that, so far, we seem not to be heeding at all, as my essay *Newspeak* shows. [22]

As great a pioneer as Jung is in his discovery of this great transformation, Giegerich points out that he, Jung, refused the final implications of what he knew to be true and retreated, living what became in fact a double life. One life was the prosaic and modern professor of Kusnacht and the other was the "age-old son of the mother" at Bollingen, immersed once again in (psychologically obsolete) historical meaning.

With all this in place we are now in a position to understand the radioactive or destructive aspect of this transformation in consciousness that is taking place: [23]

---

[22]   (Woodcock, 2011)

[23]   (Giegerich, 2010)

> *The unconscious is indeed a "casket for storage and transport of radioactive waste," as it were, but not because archetypes and Gods are allegedly still alive and thus as dangerous as radioactive materials, but only because if we, as the modern consciousness that we are, would nevertheless still believe in them and take them as present realities, we would then, and only then, be threatened by inflation or psychosis.* (266)

I can amplify Giegerich's masterful analysis in terms of my own situation with the "radioactivity" of my "atomic bomb" dream. At the time of receiving the sustained bursts of *living thinking*, I was also teaching, consulting, and leading workshops. I had a dream of speaking with blood pouring out of my mouth—blood speech! In the groups I led, there was a "crackling" atmosphere at times and synchronicities occurred frequently. People were strongly attracted to me or as strongly repelled by me. I began to imagine myself as a prophet, uttering truths and speaking of the future. My clinical work was peppered with strange happenings that produced transformation or disasters! But I had no control of the process. I was, to put it succinctly, in a dreadful cycle of inflation-deflation that bordered on psychosis, as Giegerich writes above. Soon, I withdrew from most activities that placed me in contact with the public and settled into a more introverted, withdrawn posture.

I began the long labour required to assist the alchemy of my own and our soul life.

THE NEW FORM

I can report that over the years, my health has returned and my "radiation sickness" is gone. In its place I experience at times a flow of *living thinking* that is insistent, but not violent. I can even negotiate over matters of timing (can this wait until I get home, etc.) I have remained faithful to soul life and, in return for endless hours of giving expression to soul in words, I sometimes get days or weeks off.

The words that come, or more precisely the *form* of the words that come, have led me to research genres of literature. So far, I have found nothing like it. My essay *Sewing His Own Garment* (see below in present book) explores this (possibly) new genre in which the writing moves from a memory to a dream to a reflection of an external event, to an etymological study of a word, to the words of another author until the usual separation of inner and outer dissolves. I have written several books which are expressive of this style and I am beginning to suspect that this is my task, i.e., to find a literary genre that expresses/describes our new nature as *thinking beings*, in the sense of living thinking, as I have been showing above.

It seems to me that we are each living in a historical moment as possible co-creators of form, in the way that the WORD created form, except of course, *sublated* as Giegerich teaches. In my view, understanding the process of sublation through direct experience is the sure path of avoiding or transforming the "destructive fury that lies within" (see Barfield above).

As co-creators of form we now have a responsibility that we did not have in previous historical moments in which human beings simply lived embedded within the world, as given by soul. In contrast, we now have the capacity to turn towards and to *become* the *living thinking* that appears as *other* yet is also us, and then to turn away, back towards the empirical world, rendering another aspect of our deeper soul-being into an art form, thus making a small contribution towards the next set of collective representations, or to say it prosaically, our world.

As we can readily observe, many ordinary individuals have found their way to this level of the *self-presentational* soul. This "lava flow" of *living thinking* or spontaneous stream of fantasies is occurring in individuals who have little preparation or knowledge of the process that has befallen them. For example, listen to the author of Harry Potter describing her creative process: [24]

> ... in 1990 my then boyfriend and I decided to move up to
> Manchester ... it was after a weekend's flat-hunting ...
> that the idea of Harry Potter simply fell into my head. I
> had been writing almost continuously since the age of six,
> but I had never been so excited about an idea before ...
> all the details bubbled up in my brain, and this scrawny,
> black-haired bespectacled boy who didn't know he was a
> wizard became more and more real to me.

Rowlings was suddenly catapulted into unimaginable wealth and fame and her books are surely shaping the world to come.

Many individuals today are participating in the incarnation of this or that aspect of the life of the soul, through an art or cultural form. They often do so with little discrimination beyond the pull of money, fame or power. We now are living in a world based completely on the logic of *difference*. Being different or new is what matters artistically, as tradition and centrality collapse completely. We saw the pull of power in the creation of the atomic bomb and now, sixty or so years after its detonation we are seeing even more peculiar and indeed grotesque forms entering material reality.

Under these pressing circumstances, when one set of collective representations is replacing another, (transformation of the world) we might do well to remember Owen Barfield's warning: [25]

> *Imagination is not, as some poets have thought, simply*
> *synonymous with good. It may be either good or evil. As*
> *long as art remained primarily mimetic, the evil which*
> *imagination could do was limited by nature ... [b]*

---

[24]   Found at Rowlings' official web site in 1997 but it seems no longer to be available (2012).

[25]   (Barfield O., 1962)

ut . . . when the fact of the directionally creator relation is beginning to break through into consciousness, both the good and evil latent in the working of imagination begin to appear unlimited. We have seen in the Romantic movement an instance of the way in which the making of images may react on the collective representations . . . we could very well move forward into a chaotically empty or fantastically hideous world . . .

We should remember this, when appraising the aberrations of the formally representational arts . . . in so far as they are genuine, they are genuine because the artist has in some way experienced the world he represents. And in so far as they are appreciated, they are appreciated by those who themselves are willing to make a move towards seeing the world in that way and, ultimately therefore, seeing that kind of world. We should remember this, when we see pictures of a dog with six legs emerging from a vegetable marrow or a woman with a motor-bicycle substituted for her left breast. (145-146)

We can and must do better than this. The new discovery of our spiritual natures is an occasion, not for self-aggrandisement but for a recognition that others, too, must be of the same spiritual nature and therefore *equal*. This *experience* of equality of our mutual spiritual being is the basis of conscience, or concern for the other, as Coleridge teaches us. [26] From this moral ground, when we each face the soul in its modern (logical) form, we may then freely choose to "materialize" soul images and thoughts in art or deed, on a basis of *love for the other*, rather than what seems to be happening today, on a basis of lust for *power* or *might*.

What would our collective representations look like, then?

---

[26]   (Barfield O., 1944, p. 139)

Sewing His
Own Garment

INTRODUCTION

I have consulted the *I Ching* for over twenty years. I use the yarrow stalks method of generating the hexagram which takes about twenty minutes and allows me to settle into the question. I have a kind of discipline about asking for an oracle from the *old man*. I only approach him when I feel I have run out of my own resources. This restraint is based on my rather deep conviction that wisdom can only approach when the ego is sufficiently open and transparent, able therefore to distinguish between its own concerns and the *voice of the other*. This happens to me when I truly feel I can no longer address my situation from the ego alone.

I then spend some time in formulating the question, making sure that the question does not merely reflect what I already know and secretly want affirmed. A question worthy of the *old man's* attention is one that is relatively purged of personal desire. When I have asked for an oracle in this way, the reading has profoundly affected me and the image has formed the basis of subsequent action, lasting for years before I need to ask again.

In 2006 I arrived once again at the point where I felt ready to ask for wisdom. I asked this question:

*What is my current situation (my life up til now) and
what does the future hold?*

The hexagram I received was *The Wanderer* and it had one
changing line from which emerged the hexagram of *Stillness*.
The *old man* had given me an image of my life's history up to
date and an image of what will emerge from it. In other words,
what had been a series of apparently fragmented, historical events
occurring in my outer life now had now gained the logical status
of an *image of spiritual reality*—my destiny!

This intuited connection between history (in this case, my
personal history) and soul movement (spiritual reality) is of course
the very essence of this book. Put another way, I am exploring
how an ordinary life lived in the real world of contingency, in
the stream of time known as past-future is in essence *a soul image
unfolding into existence*.

In my own case it would appear from my question and the *I
Ching* reading that my personal history is a working into existence
of the image of *The Wanderer* transforming into *Stillness*.

Can this process be *demonstrated* in some way? Can it be
shown how a series of apparently disconnected historical events
in fact form the fragments of an image working its way into
existence?

Throughout this book I have tried to articulate a
methodology of demonstrating just this process. I begin by
paying attention to certain events occurring in the world:, i.e.,
events characterized by qualities of the *unusual*, the *unfamiliar*,
the *startling* all of which obviously involve my psychological
participation, and then I open myself up to these phenomena
sufficiently for them to penetrate my consciousness, so that
I begin *to think the thought of the phenomenon*, distinct from
my thinking *about* them This process is in effect an initiation
into another form of consciousness, the consciousness of the
phenomenon. This finally can form the basis for new action
in the world, action that is not simply a repeat of the known
past but instead carries the germ of a new future. These actions

always took me away from the security of the familiar into the unknown future.

My method of writing is therefore an attempt to develop an *art form* that can demonstrate this process. I soften the boundaries of my ego and pay attention to unusual, unfamiliar, or even startling images that "arrive". I take up a relationship with these visitors and am prepared to leave my present path to follow their hints. I record this process as it goes on. A kind of *wandering* therefore takes place in my writing as in my life (see previous essays).

In this way, I move from a memory, to a dream, to a reflection of an event in the world, to an etymological study of a word, to the words of another author. I do not concern myself with any separation between inner and outer, past and future, fact and fiction, i.e., the usual categories of experience. The one constant is that all my writing springs out of the soil of immediate experience and so is real. I pay attention to detail, or hints that emerge freely from "within", no matter how small or seemingly insignificant. It takes a kind of surrender to psychic process in order to write this way, and a faith that I won't fall merely into chaos, or madness. But this is far from certain!

So, what does happen?

As I keep writing, each fragment begins to call forth another and I begin to get a definite feeling of being drawn towards a meaning, as yet hidden. A momentum starts up as I am drawn towards the unknown future. Remembered events in my life, experienced initially as fragments, gather towards an image expressive of spiritual meaning. I begin to perceive an image "appearing" within the syntax of my ordinary life.

In *this* essay I decided to remember whatever I could of my *entire* personal history, following the method of this, my art form. If I am successful then you, my reader, may be able to discern an image slowly emerging into clarity through the gathered fragments and once again, if my method is sound, in the case of my entire personal history, the image emerging into focus will be that of *The Wanderer* transforming into *Stillness*.

And so, a poem fragment begins this journey: [27]

> *Our birth is but a sleep and a forgetting:*
> *The Soul that rises with us, our life's Star,*
> *Hath had elsewhere its setting,*
> *And cometh from afar:*
> *Not in entire forgetfulness,*
> *And not in utter nakedness,*
> *But trailing clouds of glory do we come*
> *From God, who is our home:*
> *Heaven lies about us in our infancy!*
> *Shades of the prison-house begin to close*
> *Upon the growing Boy, . . .*

---

[27]　William Wordsworth: *Ode, Intimations of Immortality from Recollections of Early Childhood*

B eing born an only child is bad enough! Although the story goes that you get all this attention from your parents, the fact is you also miss out on a lot, like siblings and all the feelings and experiences that sibling relationships can bring. Unlike other "only children" however, I had to compete with the presence of several imaginary cats that my mother and stepfather included in our family. As most children do, I had a kind of innocent acceptance of the reality of these "siblings", although I did not feel part of *that* family at all. I simply accepted the fact that on occasion, my parents would speak about these cats in an atmosphere of amusement that comes with collusion in a secret—or even a *folie a deux*!

It was only years later that I was able to associate the presence of the cats to the repeated miscarriages that my mother endured as she tried to have a child with my stepfather. In the meantime I had my own little secret. It lay in the recesses of my imagination, hidden in a dark corner. I rarely approached it and asked a question. On the other hand, I never forgot about it. I simply felt and knew that in my family, a murder or some violent act had been committed. With parents who held their own closely guarded secrets, I could not expect any adequate answer to my question. Instead I followed my intuition, putting out feelers here and there.

When I was about seven or eight we lived in a small town called Redcliff, a coastal suburb of Brisbane. My stepfather owned a wooden chest which for some reason was stored in our neighbours' garage. Mum and Pop Brumby were the closest I felt to having real grandparents. I loved going over there, particularly to feed the chickens that were kept in a wire cage. It may be the only time I enjoyed weeding the garden because I was in fact collecting food for the birds. I even managed somehow to witness Pop beheading a chicken in preparation for the meal. He missed the vital point on the neck of course and so we watched as the headless monster raced frantically around the yard spilling its blood, and gargling a strangled sound as it struggled to come to terms with its new status of separation. Somehow a child can even take that horror in as simply a fact. Perhaps it is because a child really does accept life being so much more than he can possibly comprehend.

The chest lay unlocked in the garage like a pirate's treasure waiting to be plundered. My stepfather had an uncle who fought in the Boer War. The chest was in fact a war chest, filled with memories of his campaign in South Africa. I especially loved his two ceremonial swords and used them in combat with other boys over the next few years. The soft metal of the blade could not withstand the full force of our clumsy techniques and the edges grew pitted and nicked, just like a sword should look I suppose.

There were stacks of old letters in this chest and one letter he wrote told how he survived in the desert by eating the local melons that grew wild there. I was accustomed to spending hours alone in my play and this chest was a rich harvest for my imagination. Somehow the chest gave credence to my omnipresent feeling that some violence had been committed in my family. I associated the military with the violence. I also imagined cancer and prison.

Viv my stepfather was also in the army. He served in the Korean War in 1950, the year I was born. His left wrist was shattered leaving a huge scar. And he held violence in his body! I learned, as my mother did, that you don't sneak up behind him for any reason whatsoever. When my mother did once he almost laid her out with a punch. Luckily he snapped back into ordinary reality in time and the punch never landed. When I was about twelve, my mother told me that he had disappeared. A few days later he was found hundreds of miles north in Bundaberg, his birth town. He had no memory of his journey "back home". He had entered a fugue state, it seems.

My mother met Viv in Puckapunyl, Victoria. In 1951, my original family had emigrated to Australia. My father, Samuel John Woodcock, Jack, was also in the armed forces. He served in the Second World War in the African campaign and later in Sicily as a driver of amphibian vehicles. He was also a sniper. He served as a simple soldier, rising to the rank of Corporal. After the war he returned to his working class roots as a driver, this being the time he met my mother. It seems that there was some urgency in their leaving England in 1951. This sense of urgency may have had something to do with a scandal. Shortly after my mother and father were married, possibly while she was pregnant with me, my mother had apparently begun an exceedingly strange affair with Bill, Jack's brother. He called upon her and they had dated, much to the horror of her parents, my Grandparents. It's not clear to me how far they took this liaison but it did raise in my mind the question of my paternity! She did tell me many years later that she had preferred Bill all along and if her Dad (also Bill) had merely whispered "don't do it", she would have fled the wedding. All this resonates with a wedding photo I have which displays a telling gesture in my young mother's eyes: "Wait and see! You have no idea who you have married!"

Jack enlisted in the Australian Army through a London office which of course provided us with immediate accommodation and some measure of financial security and so we all quickly left town. We arrived in Puckapunyl in July 1951 on board the ship *Otranto*.

Four years later, Jack's meticulous army record which I obtained only in 2005 held a strange evocative note: "Application for Transfer: For urgent personal and domestic reasons . . ."

Viv was my father's best friend and he had had an affair with my mother. He waited until Jack left for Melbourne one day and fled with my mother and me. Jack returned, discovered his monumental loss through a double betrayal, grabbed a loaded pistol and chased them. Perhaps this was what Viv and Gwen feared. Jack was a soldier. He had seen action and was a sniper. In his young man's naiveté he had been betrayed by his best friend and his young wife. He had murder in his heart. He somehow managed to retrieve me without killing anyone and returned to his barracks where his commanding officer convinced him to give me back.

I never saw my dad again.

I do have a strange residual memory of that period that surfaced again right now, as I write:

"My mother and Viv are going somewhere together and are leaving me at a home. There is a large white rabbit in the yard. I am playing with him". I now wonder if that memory is showing me a possible path I took to deal with the intense suffering around and in me. Was I like Alice who followed the white rabbit down a hole into Wonderland?

We relocated to Redcliff in Queensland and when I was about seven years old my mother told me that I was to have a new surname, that of my stepfather and so I was legally adopted by him. When I was twenty one, i.e., as soon as I was legally able, my mother took me to a solicitor so that I could change my name by Deed Poll, permanently. She was determined that all ties with my father were to be severed. I did so meekly, not having the faintest idea about the struggle that had been going on around me for so many years.

The only leverage my father had to get me back was to withhold his permission for a divorce and he had done so for another ten years until in the early 1960's when he finally returned to England. My mother therefore could not marry Viv. In return for having her will thwarted, she blocked any correspondence from Jack to me. Whenever his name came up, she became filled with scorn and hatred. I came to "know" my father only through the prejudicial eyes of my mother, except for that small persistent intuition that violence or maybe even a murder had been committed in my family . . .

In 1973, I had completed my post graduate training as a teacher and was shortly thereafter to embark on an ambitious project of starting up my own school—*The Orwell School*—which became the first secondary alternative school in Queensland. During that period, my mother asked me to come with her to

England to visit her mother and so, once again meekly, I did. This trip had the unintended (by me) consequence of further sundering my connection with my blood relatives—this time on my mother's side, through, once again, my mother's agency.

Somehow the old hatred between my mother and *her* mother erupted once again and somehow I became thoroughly entangled in it though I never knew the content of the dispute. Venom spilled out towards me and my grandmother's refusal to give me the traditional inheritance from my grandfather Bill. His gold watch and other objects were to be passed on to the eldest grandson. I was effectively disinherited in that small act.

My mother's sisters did write to me from time to time, after that incident, especially Pat who lived in South Africa. I found a kindred soul in her eventually, after another twenty-five years, but in the meantime I was cast off from the warmth of blood ties on both my mother's and father's side.

My state of disinheritance, and alienation from my relatives was completed in 1998 when my mother died of cancer. Her Will provided entirely for her latest husband and I received nothing. To this day I know nothing of my mother's financial standing. This knowledge was also hidden from me throughout my life with her. I suspect very strongly that the main reason for disinheriting me arose from my decision in 1994 to legally change my name back to Woodcock, my birth name. She was infuriated when I told her.

At the time, the painful stripping away of my connections to ordinary life was deepening considerably. I was being opened up to invisible realities and bursting forth with poetry, essays and other creative forms that could give expression to these encounters. I was so captivated by my discoveries that I did not notice how marginalized and alienated I was becoming. I felt that my old life was over and that nothing would remain. After much struggle I arrived at a point of choice where the option of remaining here at all became viable.[28]

---

[28]   (Woodcock, 2009)

My choice to remain and forge a new beginning was symbolized by my claiming my birth right symbolized by my father's name. I legally changed my name and my first important social act with my new name was to become a citizen of the United States as John C. Woodcock.

As with so many fundamental shifts in my life, my return to ordinary life and the restoration of my family ties began with a dream. It was the year 2002 and I was lying on the couch as usual, in a state of depression. I spent many hours on that couch—the very couch on which my son had been born. For the past several years I had been engaged in a struggle to return to ordinary life. My efforts included Ph.D. studies and getting a permanent job in an institution, the first in twenty years. I felt new significance in ordinary life and this led to a feeling of urgency. It was more than personal survival. I had developed a deep conviction that my experiences in the wasteland would be, well, wasted if I could not achieve a return. Yet all my efforts seemed to get thwarted. I could not avoid a personal bankruptcy and I could not avoid having to sell my home—prime real estate—within a year of buying it. It seemed to me that mighty forces were marshalled against me and that I would surely fail. I simply did not see at the time that these dreadful events together constituted the very mechanism of returning to ordinary life.

During my hours on the couch I alternated between watching TV and falling asleep. In the early hours of the morning, I woke suddenly hearing a voice, a woman's voice. She simply spoke my name: John! With the uncanny certainty that comes with intuition, I knew that I was being approached by something new, yet familiar, and that I would emerge from my current despair. I knew equally that I must be attentive to small signs and be ready to follow the hint.

The dream was startling enough but even more so as I remembered my experiences in Detroit, Michigan between 1998 and 1999, the time I completed my Ph.D. This was also the time I entered a short-lived marriage which seemed to be the instrument through which unimaginable forces were funnelled, appearing as insurmountable obstacles to my attempts to return to ordinary life.

I now understand that they may have been the very forces required to strengthen me for that return, to in fact create a lighthouse (see *Lighthouse at the End of the World*).

I named this time my Nightmare. My fear moved into terror and yet the only guidance I received from my inner world or from outer assistance came in the form of one word—courage! I had no hope and hovered near despair. I felt cut off from everything that supported my life. In the middle of this torment my mentor sent me an e-mail in which he simply suggested I listen to a particular song. It is a song (by Enya) taken from the movie: *The Last of the Mohicans*. The song's lyrics include, "I will find you if it takes a thousand years . . ."

Four years later as I woke up on my couch, startled by the dream voice, a woman's voice, I could only conclude that she had found me and that my connection to the psyche, which had been broken by too much fear, was now restored.

I began once again to follow the hints of my psyche as a path into the future.

Several months later in March 2003, I was surfing the Internet, seeing what possible avenues of employment there may be for a recent graduate in the relatively new field of Consciousness Studies. On an impulse I decided to look up a friend from Australia who I knew was working at a university in Sydney. I e-mailed him and while I was at it, I asked if he knew the e-mail address of one Anita Hansen. He kindly sent it to me after first asking her, and I quickly wrote to her. Anita was my great and confused love in Australia, before I left for the USA in 1979. It was also her image that appeared to me at the start of my Ph.D. program (see essay, *Lighthouse at the End of the World*). She had actually visited me several times in the U.S.A. as our lives unfolded in a startlingly parallel way. For example, we were separated from our marriages at the same time. We circled around each other, much as we had done while in Australia. Now we made contact and it was a strong one.

We were both ready!

Within three months I sold my home, paid most of my debts, gave notice at my employment and paid for two one-way tickets for me and my son. We arrived in Sydney and my return to ordinary life was suddenly free of all resistance.

This path I took was the only one that remained open to me and it was the only one I wanted to choose. All other doors closed firmly and without regret. When this happens I know with a certainty that there is congruence, a "oneness" between inner and outer existence.

In 2005, two years after settling back in Australia and one year after marrying my Anita, I woke up with a memory of having been "somewhere" last night. In other words, I experienced continuity between my sleeping and waking state, in contrast to the normal event of waking up remembering dreams that seem to bear no relationship to one's waking state. It had the character of my being shown something real:

> I am enfolded by an angelic being who gazes at me with great love and we rise off the ground to the heights of vision. He has the face of Rudolph Steiner. My eyes are directed towards the horizon and I see an ominous and menacing dark cloud approaching—this is our future—it is inevitable and just so. My eyes are then directed away from this foreboding vision to one side where I see a bustling harbor, full of commerce and trade. The word "prosperity" comes and I know this is a premonition of my personal future, taking place on a small scale within the larger vision of possible global catastrophe.

This was a crucial dream-vision for me because, during the 80's and 90's I had been immersed in visions of possible futures and could find no reason to go on in the face of such dire warnings. Here I was shown the possibility of going on, even prospering in the personal sphere while holding the knowledge of a larger impersonal menace in the background.

It was also exceedingly interesting to me that "prosper" springs from the same root as "despair". They are two sides of the same coin! In temporal terms it seemed to me that I had moved down through despair to the seed of prosperity. My mentor also reminded me that prosperity associates to *Prospero* from *The Tempest*. This was quite exciting to me because for years, well before my dream of prosperity I had been drawn to a song by Loreena McKennitt who puts the closing speech of Prospero into musical form:

prospero's speech

Now my charms are all o'erthrown,
And what strength I have's mine own,
Which is most faint: now, 'tis true,
I must be here confined by you . . .
But release me from my bands
With the help of your good hands:
Gentle breath of yours my sails
Must fill, or else my project fails,
Which was to please.
Now I want Spirits to enforce, art to enchant,
And my ending is despair,
Unless I be relieved by prayer,
Which pierces so that it assaults
Mercy itself and frees all faults.
As you from crimes would pardon'd be,
Let your indulgence set me free.

Prospero here is recounting his journey from disinheritance and banishment to an island where, although isolated from his heritage and rightful position as Duke of Naples, he gains mastery over magical powers. His condition of alienation opens him to invisible influences. When his place in society is restored, he relinquishes his powers in favour of becoming ordinary again ("what strength I have's mine own"). He even speaks of the despair that can come if that return is impeded. He seems to recognize that being on that island in the play is like being in a dream. One may "wake up" to the fact that one is in a dream state and yet still run the risk of being caught in that state. The applause of the audience is required to "break the spell". One cannot do that oneself. At the time of my own fascination with this beautiful poem rendered in song I had not reflected in this way at all. Only when my mentor broke the spell for me by naming the prospero-complex, could I be free to view it from the outside. I could only then gain some knowledge of what I had been through.

My own prosperic return to ordinary life was accomplished by getting the only job that opened up for me, as a mathematics teacher at a Catholic School in Sydney, in 2004 when I had just recently returned from the USA.

How often a new chapter opens up for me through the appearance of a single, unfamiliar door when all others, based on my past experiences, remain closed to me!

The concerns of school life were so alien to the realities I had been immersed in for so long yet I was forced to engage them. Indeed, I found that "what strength I have's mine own". Many times I felt unequal to the task. The very way I *languaged* the world was alien to what was expected of me on a daily basis. So I discovered that I had been placed in the very context most fitted for re-entry into a world that was proceeding as if the invisible psyche did not exist. And for the first time in about twenty years, I had enough money to prosper.

From within that daily grind a seed grew.

I decided to renew my search for my father . . .

I still had some photos of my childhood and one of them was taken as my parents and I sailed from England to Victoria in 1951. On the back of the old black and white image, my mother had scrawled the name of the ship, *Otranto*. This detail arose along with the curious discovery that I had a cousin on my mother's side living in Sydney. Lee was the youngest son of Pat, my mother's sister. I had been corresponding with Pat ever since my mother died. She was the only relative who immediately responded to my account of life with my mother. Her own story was equally disturbing and together we gained a mutually satisfying picture of my mother's complex nature and its effects on each of us.

Through Pat and her husband David, I found my way to Anne, also my cousin who had taken on the task of recovering the family tree on my maternal side. She and her mother Pat told me that they had tried for years to find my dad, Jack, with no luck. I learned that when he had returned to England in 1961, after my mother disappeared with Viv and me up north, he stayed with Pat and David for a while and was considered part of the family. Then they had lost contact.

All this recently acquired news rekindled my own enthusiasm for finding my father and I began to follow these new trails. The Internet of course has become a valuable resource for locating relatives, living or dead. It seems that discovering one's origins has become a matter of considerable importance to millions of dispossessed individuals these days.

But all trails dried up because I lacked a crucial piece of information—my dad's birth date or maybe his death date. The fact that I had changed my name back to my father's name in 1994 of course eased matters considerably. If I had kept my adopted name, so many doors would have remained closed because of the social issue of adoption and locating biological parents. At least bureaucracy was listening to me, but I could not provide the crucial data to get me into the system until my lovely wife stepped in. Anita is a social worker working for the Veterans Department of the Australian Government. She obtained my father's Army records from the Australian Army. The barriers dissolved. Soon I received a thick folder of meticulously kept records of my father's career in the armed forces of Australia.

From these records I learned of the double betrayal my dad endured in 1955 and which probably resulted in his hospitalization with depression. For the first time in my life I gained impressions of him that were not conditioned by my mother's hatred. And I obtained his birth date! From there I entered the British *Registry of Births and Deaths* to discover that he died only a few months before I had begun my search, i.e., on May 15 2005. Curiously my mother had died on May 14, 1998, seven years earlier.

I had missed my dad by only a few months.

I found out that he died at Worcestershire Hospital from complications arising from a lifetime of smoking. He developed gangrene and at his age it was inoperable. I called the hospital and a kindly social worker assisted me in locating the funeral home which had taken care of his burial. I talked with an employee there who struggled with releasing any information over the phone but did tell me his next of kin: his wife's name was Gwendolyn! I almost dropped the phone. That is my mother's name. I felt instant confusion. Why would he name my mother as next of kin? I blurted out that my mother's name is Gwendolyn and my informant seemed unsurprised since I had identified myself as his son. She went on to drop another bombshell. Who arranged his funeral service? Why, his daughter did.

Within a few days of discovering my dad had died I discovered I have a living sister, whose mother, it turned out, was also called Gwendolyn.

The funeral director of course would not release any details over the phone but by now I was unstoppable. I found out my dad lived his remaining years in Droitwich and simply by looking in the local phone book via the Internet, I found one Jim Woodcock who indeed was my last living uncle. My father had three brothers and one sister and now only Jim is left (2005). We struck up an immediate friendship and it turned out Jim had completed a lot of work on the Woodcock lineage. He also told me more about my sister and also about Jack's marriage, which seemed in an uncanny way to be a repeat of his and my mother's. When I did finally talk to my sister we had an immediate and strong connection with surprisingly similar descriptions of our mothers.

More than this though, over the following weeks my cousins and various nephews and nieces appeared in a kind of avalanche. I was welcomed into the family like a long lost son. I scrambled to construct a family tree so I wouldn't forget who belonged to whom. One particular touching moment emerged when one cousin sent me a photo of myself, about five years old, that she had kept all this time. More photos and stories came from Jim and my sister. I felt like a ship that had been listing to one side and suddenly was righted. I felt quite disoriented in a most pleasant way. My self-image was being drastically altered under the amazing onslaught of love and kindness extended to me from all my relatives.

I am no longer an "only child". I am no longer "fatherless". I have an extended family. I am a brother to someone and I am Uncle John to some young people. I have a history that others know about and respond to. I remember the small shock I received as I perused my dad's Army records and saw where he listed me as his son. There it was in black and white, a record of my presence in my father's psyche.

My sister told me that I was never forgotten. Although Jack was afraid to talk about me to his wife, he never forgot me and in fact Uncle Jim told me that they both initiated a long search for me over the years, without success. I had lived in the Woodcock memory during my time of banishment and disinheritance and in fact for my entire life . . .

From the 1970's through the nineties, the garments with which we move through life, which clothe us from birth on with our cultural identity were stripped away from me, sometimes in the most painful way. I had dreams in which I appear naked, trying to express my truth in public and being chased away; dreams in which clothing did not fit, was lost or was from my past, no longer fitting me. These soul realities corresponded with my not knowing how to function adequately in the world. I dreamed of being flayed, sitting on a chair in a dark basement; or, of a body being stripped down to the bones by sharks. I was being reduced to a soul condition which prepares the soul for a direct encounter with spiritual realities.

I found employment where I could, never feeling I belonged anywhere, always "trying on clothing" that did not fit me or in some way distorted what I really wanted to say. I entered different professions, only to leave or get tossed out. My creative impulses were channelled into social forms that were already conserved in regulations or traditions and so I always felt distorted. Although I "performed" well at whatever I put my hand to, nowhere did I feel "at home".

I was a wanderer.

At the same time, I was opened to the spirit. The "removal of garments" was for me a living symbol for stripping away my attachments to outer life. I did not go easily into that good night. For years I was almost obsessive about keeping documentation about my legal and social identity (passport, Deed Poll, birth certificate, professional licenses, academic transcripts, degrees, letters of recommendation which were over ten years old, brochures of my workshops, lectures, and on and on) while at the same time I became more and more alienated from the community. I lost my marriage, went into bankruptcy, lost my home, gave up my professional licenses, refused to work in any institution, so was mostly broke, and lost all connection with my family on both sides.

I wrote a poem expressing this condition:

until I surrender

living a life of hopeful anticipation
but the foundation of the house was rotten
bursts of scattering activity
plunges into mindless blackness
edifice crumbles at last

clutching to possessions
thieves come in the night
room laid bare
grasp at career
guard dogs bare their teeth
no entry here

family and home
slowly debts
the weight of saturn
cast into lead

now my son visits during the week
weeds grow head high on the land
office built with my own hands
stands empty

no family no career no community
husband father professional teacher writer
all gone
discredited
unwanted
inadequate

all failures

wind accepts the offering of my wallet
left carelessly on the roof of my car
there goes my identity
turning to my body and psyche
instruments of pleasure for others
never mine at all

nothing left

yet more to hang onto
dreams feelings memories
concepts of reality
god as a concept
merciless insistence!
these are taken too

sitting in the front seat
bowed over the wheel
despair
nowhere to go
crazy mexican breaks into my truck
looking into his eyes
I see what i do not want to see
nobody home!
he returns later to finish the job
let him go
he must be god's angel

lying on my back
beyond despair
now well into sheer terror

abyss opens up below
crying out to mother for support
there is … something
point dot hypothesis

brief excursion into the beyond
yields a non-dimensional
but real other
my very existence is now based
on this tiniest of tinies

how the merest terror-filled glimpse
into the abyss
can yield so much!
quite an achievement!
i get the point
only to miss it entirely
still clinging to heroic knowledge

and so you come

what despair and terror began
love completes
you love me until i surrender

abyss . . . is life!
i know not
but i love

This poem is only one of an outpouring of creative impulses that lasted several years. I was in an ecstatic ferment and worked hard to give expression to the mighty flow that had started up and intensified the more I was marginalized. The more I was stripped away of any garments that society had made for me, the more I was opened up to direct encounters with spiritual reality.

I have made many attempts to express and interpret what was happening to me and one such attempt may be found in my book: *Making of a Man: Initiation through the Divine Mother.*[29] Here is an excerpt from that book:

> *For weeks I experienced a flooding of my body with a kind of nectar that produced an ecstasy in me. I could smell flowers or sweet fragrance in the air. I felt I had grown a pair of wings, palpably, concretely. The erotic intensity was such that I would lay down for hours as a fount of glorious liquid fire poured into me. Many dreams came, and visions, too many to recount here but the flood swept away everything that I had so far assumed about life, the human condition and its limitations. I was given experiences of a concrete nature, whose reality could not be questioned at all and yet which could not possibly be reduced or interpreted back into known categories of experience.*

---

[29]   (Woodcock, 2012)

These ecstasies were expressions of a spiritual reality that wished to enter the human experience. My life since these times has been an attempt to concretize this reality in the ordinary context of my own life. I have felt this as an "evolutionary task" for many years, aided by the many dreams which offered hints of this meaning or destiny. In one such dream:

> *I am offered a glass filled with champagne and small rocks which I drank fully down—the most spiritual and the most commonplace together in the one vessel, assimilated in one ordinary life.*

These experiences taught me of my spiritual origins, that there is a spiritual aspect of my human totality that belongs to and has emerged from the spiritual realms and is at home there. I also learned that making this discovery while embodied can involve the most terrible suffering. In our incarnate state our desires are directed outwards in the service of life, albeit unconscious life. When we are turned inwards reality also turns inside out and so desire appears on the outside directed towards us. I thus discovered myself as an object of desire—desire as an image, and I was stripped of any garb that would direct my attention to the outer material world. Thus I was shown the true state of affairs. Becoming an object of desire involves interpenetrating with spiritual powers whilst having a finite body. Suffering thus is the experience of a limited being filled by these powers.

My return to my familial origins was thus in effect a "return from the dead". Not only had I discovered my spiritual origins from above (the future), but now I was reunited with my blood origins, from below (the past). These two streams were re-uniting in me in a way that produced some very difficult effects.

Throughout 2006, I had a series of dreams that showed me trying to do my work in the world but having great difficulty finding the right clothes to wear. I try on clothes from my own past, clothes that belong to others, none of which fit. I found this very frustrating in the dreams. I could not get on with my "work" as a teacher. I also had a remarkable dream which linked my own participation in an incarnation process with that of one Walter Benjamin. The dream showed that a book comprised entirely of quotations had been completed. Following the dream I was startled to read that Walter Benjamin had spent his life collecting quotes just as I had and he wanted to create such a book, without commentary. The idea underlying such a creative activity is this: modern life is in fragments but with a proper attitude (he called it the *flâneur*) he could gather fragments to himself in such a way as to reveal the hidden thread linking them and placing them uniquely in this historical moment. In this way the shattered meaning underlying the fragmentation in our modern life could be revealed to the flâneur.

From these dream hints I began to see the movement in my own life in a fresh way that was quite depressing. I had a wealth of visionary material within, waiting as it were to find its way into world, pressing hard upon me, in fact, heating my body, and leaving my skin in a painful itching condition that was unbearable at times.

On the other hand my outer life had been reduced to the bones and any attempt to return to outer forms that were conserved (from the past) or which belonged to others was thwarted by a deeper intentionality. I had all the raw material, but how to bring it into the world? The necessity to do so was clear. I dreamed of assisting a birth—a baby was born and there was a rush of enthusiasm. He came in fresh and pink and naked—a beautiful birth. Then immediately I dreamed of an uncompromising death. A black and white bird appears as a judge over life and death and an animal carcass falls from the sky, without its skin. Could this be what was left after a *sublimatio* process, and which had to go to its animal death? An animal dies and a human is born. This is an image of a transformation.

My depression deepened as my skin condition worsened over the months. The death image in my dreams also alarmed me. In my outer world, I concluded that I would not seek any other job in an institution, or rework my resume one more time, in order to distort myself to fit an institution. I would not try to fit myself in any other clothes. My present job as a mathematics teacher at the Catholic school was a temporary gift to me, helping me stabilize financially and the holidays that came with the job gave me the time to reflect and work on my inner life. It would be my last position within any organization.

With all the hints from my dreams I was stymied, unable to rely on past forms to bring in my spiritual reality and not knowing how else to proceed or where to turn for help.

During all this uncertainty, I continued to deepen my connection with my sister and with my ancestral line. With Uncle Jim's considerable help, I found my way to one Henry MacDonald in the USA. He was a distant cousin who had traced his own line back into the Woodcocks and even posted it on his website. In another strange turn of events, it turned out he lived in the Seattle area where I had lived for twenty years without knowing of his existence. With his and Jim's help I was able to construct a family line back to the 18th century. My son Chris and I descend from an all-male line starting from one Daniel Woodcock, born 1778. His son was Samuel Woodcock, whose wife gave birth to eleven children. Five died within the first two years of their lives, one of whom was named John Woodcock. My ancestors mostly lived in Chester, England, or around the Midlands as my dad did.

Uncle Jim sent me an old photo of my great-great-grandfather, Samuel Woodcock standing out in front of his shop with some of his children and perhaps his wife. Standing there in front of his little shop in Chester, Samuel portrays those last remaining vestiges of human dignity captured so well in 19th century portraits (see photo above).

As with my parents' wedding photo this one was very psychoactive for me. But it took months for me to realize that the most obvious feature of this photo held a mystery that was very relevant to my own life as I had struggled to give it form over these many years of "banishment" from and return to my father's family.

I have known for some time, through listening to others' stories of their own families, that there is a special bond between grandparent and grandchild. They are at the opposite ends of the human life span. The child is just "coming in" as it were, and the grandparent is on his "way out". So they each can relate to each other in their spiritual beings. The grandparent often in fact transmits something of the spirit freely to the grandchild, a gift, unencumbered by the usual parental concerns that produce conflicts between the child's spiritual freedom and the necessary limitations of material existence. A grandchild can thus find an undiscovered meaning in his own soul life, laid out in the enthusiasms of the grandparent's life.

So, here I am, struggling over the years to face the consequences of having my outer attachments stripped away, exposing me to spiritual treasures and at the same time enormous dangers, while being turned inside out. This process was captured as I said in images of having my clothing taken away, appearing naked, etc., followed by a return in which I was faced with my utter poverty and destitution and nakedness in bringing back some of the treasure to material life. This was portrayed in my dreams with images of clothing—unable to wear clothes from the past, trying unsuccessfully to wear clothes belonging to others, and so on.

And there is my dapper little great-great-grandfather standing so dignified, with his children and wife, in front of his little shop in Chester. The shop front says "J. Woodcock" and under that his occupation: *Tailor*!

My ancestor was a tailor! The penny drops!

My imagination began to weave around this extraordinary connection I had made with my ancestor the tailor. I returned to the photograph and saw another astonishing detail. Next to him is a little boy with a suitcase as if he were about to embark on some sort of voyage or adventure. My psyche was excited by the connection between the tailor and a voyage or journey or adventure. I knew that his son William had travelled to the USA and that my grandfather was a sailor, a submariner, to be exact. My father also was an adventurer, traveller, and indeed so am I.

I then remembered my long interest in fairy tales that feature a little tailor. In particular I loved Grimm's version. I had wondered for years what qualities the tailor possesses that the human soul uses for its own purposes, i.e., to express soul qualities interpenetrating with other soul qualities within the dramatic structure of a story. I went once again to the Internet and found this version of *The Valiant Little Tailor*: [30]

> *A tailor is preparing to eat some jam, but when flies settle on it, he kills seven of them with one blow. He makes a belt describing the deed, "Seven with one blow". Inspired, he sets out into the world to seek his fortune. The tailor meets a giant, who assumes that "Seven with one blow" refers to seven men. The giant challenges the tailor. When the giant squeezes water from a boulder, the tailor squeezes water (or whey) from cheese. The giant throws a rock far into the air, and it eventually lands. The tailor counters the feat by releasing a bird that flies away; the giant believes the small bird is a "rock" which is thrown so far that it never lands. The giant asks the tailor to help carry a tree. The tailor directs the giant to carry the trunk, while the tailor will carry the branches. Instead, the tailor climbs on, so the giant carries him as well.*
>
>   *The giant brings the tailor to the giant's home, where other giants live as well. During the night, the giant attempts to kill the man. However, the tailor, having found the bed too large, sleeps in the corner. On seeing him still alive, the other giants flee.*
>
>   *The tailor enters the royal service, but the other soldiers are afraid that he will lose his temper some day, and then seven of them might die with every blow. They tell the king that either the tailor leaves military service, or they will. Afraid of being killed by sending him away, the king instead sends the tailor to defeat two giants, offering him half his kingdom*

---

[30]   (Grimm, 2007)

and his daughter's hand in marriage. By throwing rocks at the two giants while they sleep, the tailor provokes the pair into fighting each other. The king then sends him after a unicorn, but the tailor traps it by standing before a tree, so that when the unicorn charges, he steps aside and it drives its horn into the trunk. The king subsequently sends him after a wild boar, but the tailor traps it in a chapel.

With that, the king marries him to his daughter. His wife hears him talking in his sleep and realizes that he is merely a tailor. Her father the king promises to have him carried off. A squire warns the tailor, who pretends to be asleep and calls out that he has done all these deeds and is not afraid of the men behind the door. Terrified, they leave, and the king does not try again.

In this story, the image of the little tailor gathers around a certain quality of consciousness that is extolled as a power capable of overcoming brute forces of nature, by turning them against themselves, or by trickery and deception—a kind of magical process. He sews a girdle that reads "Seven at one stroke" which has a magical effect on his adversaries. This is coupled with an irrepressible confidence in his own abilities that seems to defy his diminutive stature, delicate features, and his utter frailty in the face of overwhelming nature forces.

The tailor profession emerged in the Middle Ages and tailor guilds grew in strength and influence from that time, corresponding with a shift in culture, away from merely concealing the body (an object of shame for medieval consciousness) to accentuating various aspects of the human form (the Renaissance) or expressing one's station in life (class consciousness), or one's power and influence in the world, to the modern emphasis on fashion and *haute couture*. Tailors thus became and remain highly influential in society.

And what is it that the little tailor actually does? What magic does he weave with his needle and thread, an art whose secrets were so jealously guarded by the guilds? Grimm's fairy tale gives us a hint about what form of consciousness is involved. Perhaps Parmenides can also give us a hint . . .

When Odysseus overcomes Polythemis, the monocular giant, he does so with a form of consciousness that the Greeks named *mêtis*. As the story goes, Polythemis cries out "Who has wounded me"? Odysseus replies "No Man" and so when the giant's brothers ask, Polythemis replies, "*No Man* has wounded me". So they go away thinking him mad, enabling Odysseus and his remaining men to escape. Odysseus is exercising mêtis!

There is no way I can describe mêtis adequately, but I can sketch small hints of its centrality in human existence by drawing from a magnificent exposition of the master of mêtis, Parmenides, by Peter Kingsley: [31]

> *Mêtis was the term for cunning, skilfulness, practical intelligence; and especially for trickery. It was what could make humans, at the most basic and down-to-earth level, equal to the gods. Mêtis might sound like just another concept. But really it was the opposite of everything we understand by concepts. It meant a particular quality of intense awareness that manages to stay focused on the whole; on the lookout for hints, however subtle, for guidance in whatever form it happens to take, for signs of the route to follow however quickly they might appear or disappear.*
>
> *And in the world of mêtis there is no neutral ground, no second chance. The more you let yourself become part of it, the more you begin to discover that absolutely everything, including the fabric of reality itself, is trickery and illusion. Either you learn to stay alert or you will be led astray. There is no pause for rest, or hesitating, in between. (90)*

Mêtis is strongly associated with the image of journeying or wandering, as in Odysseus who wandered for twelve years after the

---

Trojan War. Parmenides also was a wandering traveller. Whereas Odysseus travels throughout the Mediterranean, Parmenides travelled to the realm of the goddess, through mastery of the art of incubation. But both needed mêtis.

> *As any Greek knew, the only way of steering horses or a chariot—or a ship across the ocean—was through mêtis. To be able to steer one had to know all the tricks of the road or the sea, to be watching, completely in the moment. Allowing one's mind to wander was not allowed.*
>
> *There is a good reason why the imagery of journeying is so important for the language of mêtis. It's because of the speed involved. There is the absolute need to keep focused in spite of the way everything is constantly changing, or appearing to change . . .* (91)
>
> *Whatever mêtis touches is graced with such precision that it rarely seems neat and tidy . . . it looks for certainty in the realm of uncertainty, not anywhere else; is always heading into the heart of danger.*
>
> *And the reality the goddess is pointing us to is not some safe haven of the senses. She is showing us how to steer our way through the ocean of existence, how to navigate a world riddled with cunning and deception—how to find stillness in the middle of movement, the proof of oneness in apparent separation* (94)

And finally:

> *Mêtis is the one thing needed if we are going to travel such a dangerous path without being destroyed by the forces we encounter* (437)

So here it is, in one profound concept, images of trickery, deception, illusion, along with journeying, wandering, and encountering dangerous forces, and the possibility of finding the stillness that is reality.

When I asked the *I Ching* about my path through life, it gave me the hexagram of *The Wanderer* from which emerges *The Mountain*, or *Stillness*. Mêtis is the form of consciousness that belongs to this configuration and thus my own life and at the same time, the unconscious psyche gathers all these same images around the figure of the little tailor as told in the fairy tale, as if to say that mêtis belongs there, too, with him!.

What is it about the tailor that gathers such a profound concept as mêtis around him, as displayed in Grimm's fairy tale? I believe that it is the tailor as a master form maker that gives us a clue here. With the tailor's skill we can become anything, anyone. A stitch here, a tuck there, a clever fold and suddenly an illusion is created. But only the tailor knows how and his secrets were well guarded in the guilds. Mêtis is the power informing this skill, a power that resides in goddess wisdom, a wisdom long forgotten and dismissed by our culture.

A master of mêtis, such as Parmenides and the little tailor can both create form and see through it to the stillness that is reality.

And surely the Master is one who can sew his own garments!

While I was undergoing the question of "what to wear", i.e., what form to adopt in order to incarnate the fruit of my own spiritual research, I had this extraordinary dream:

> *Lying with Anita, I enter the in-between place consciously. I observe myself with the Dalai Lama. He is on his throne and I am on a chair, looking into each other's eyes. I look deeply into his, great dark wells. There is nobody there, no form. I feel a momentary terror. Then I feel compassion pouring out of that place of emptiness. I am given a mantra: compassion flows through emptiness.*

And of course the Dalai Lama wears all the trappings of his office, the spiritual leader of the Tibetans and the leader of the exiled Tibetan Government. I suddenly felt a little closer to that ancient wisdom expressed in the Heart Sutra:

Form is Emptiness, Emptiness is Form!

I no longer doubt that I am being gifted with a considerable wisdom concerning the nature of form and the consciousness responsible for form through the agency of my ancestor the little tailor. In my own journey from wandering to stillness, I am being taught how to "sew my own garment" in contrast to trying on this or that clothing belonging to the past or to others or to this or that profession. Yet I now know that even those attempts belong to mêtis:

> . . . *Homer's hero Odysseus—the master of mêtis and cunning "who knew how to be together with people in many different ways."* (485)

I even now begin to understand my inveterate habit of quoting others, like Peter Kingsley here, as an exercise in mêtis—adopting his clothing for a while, so that I can converse in that language. Adopting and at the same time seeing through: mêtis!

But the only one who can sew his own garment is of course the tailor, a master of mêtis. I consider this image a great gift from my great-great-grandfather.

I think I am learning now that adopting this or that garb for a while, in order to converse with others is not the problem. Rather, *identifying* with the garb through attachment is a problem because I have then become a victim of mêtis and the wanderer has become lost in illusion. Neither is the issue to dispense with all clothing for that move is to deny the life affirming quality of mêtis. Rather, I can now begin to play with the image of sewing one's own garment.

This image has had immediate consequences in my life. I feel as if a long search has come to a close. I falsely believed that I was searching for the right form in which I could do my work in the world. This belief kept me in a state of frustration as the form invariably proved to be too tight, ill-fitting, odd-looking etc, distorting what I felt I had to teach. Yet, at the same time I was unconsciously engaging in exactly the right activities that express the gift of my ancestor, the art of practicing mêtis.

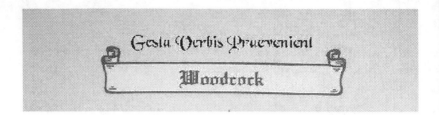

EPILOGUE

E ach essay in this book attempts to show a connection between certain contingent events in the world and the soul. Unusual, unfamiliar, even startling events can become (with the psychological participation of the observer) fragments of soul life, thereby opening the observer up to meaning. These events, when taken up by consciousness are of course fundamentally historical in nature and thus may be considered as shards, fragments of the soul in its journey towards finding itself in existence. In my last essay, *Sewing His Own Garments*, I tried to develop a literary art form that mirrors the process of discovering soul meaning emerging from the shards of an *entire* personal history, i.e., my own history.

In this epilogue I find myself grappling perhaps with a question for the future. If the content of history (from isolated events in a personal life to the great sweep of humanity's history) has no absolute meaning, i.e., can be constantly revised and improved or scrapped, then it appears that historical content (the trees) as such is not what is significant for the soul as much as the historical perspective (the forest) itself. We could even call our modern consciousness *historical consciousness* since we can do no other than comprehend ourselves as historical beings—we understand ourselves in historical terms (theory of evolution, etc.)

Over a period of years (2008-2012) I began to have a series of "death dreams" which brought this issue of being an historical consciousness into sharp focus. A question formed:

What happens when historical consciousness becomes conscious of itself? What happens when history (the forest) becomes conscious of its historical nature?

What follows is a presentation, in my chosen art form, of this question. The protagonist is named David who appears in all my books as my fictional self.

And with this last art piece, I will, like Prospero take my leave of you, my reader:

Let your indulgence set me free.

Once a human self has been emancipated from instinct to the extent of being fully aware of its own existence—if it then seeks to resume its unity with the Divine Mind, it first has to die.

The Meggid

David lay there quietly. He was dying. And he knew it. All resistance was gone now. His exposed brain was thoroughly infected with the bacteria that had rapidly invaded through his nose, once the meninges had broken down.

He "knew" it was coming, he had been warned after all. It's just that dreams emerge from a *reality* that does not easily translate into predictions in this, our ordinary reality. The meaning can go in many directions at once. These dreams had a particular emphasis on 'physicality', and death. David had felt alarmed upon awakening. With good reason, as it turned out! He had dreamed:

> *I notice my right leg. It is almost eaten away around the bone which is quite exposed. Flesh is hanging off. It has obviously been this way for some time. Well, there is no going for work now. That is over! I am under a tree and a dog comes, sniffing. He goes for my leg. At first I am alarmed then realize it is only food for him. A horse comes by. Now, some people come. They are from the organisation that assists with the passage across. I am relieved and I start weeping. Memories come and I finally remember my son Chris. I wish he were here but that is not to be. I lie there quietly.*
>
> *I see a skull. It is mine but how can that be? As I turn it slowly in my hands I marvel at how at one time my brain was in there. Now the time is close and I feel my breath going. I ask to be taken under the tree to go quietly.*

And then the second dream:

> *I decide to kill myself. A bullet in the head, but it does not kill me only knocks out brain functions. So now I am alive but in a very different way. I see Viv, (who killed himself) who tells me that meningitis is next. I move into a flat in an inner city area, almost slum where I will*

become the "Sage of Underwood" or some such. Kate, the
actress from Underbelly sings nearby to me and the song
is beautiful; just beautiful.

When David gathered himself enough to reflect, he noticed
the definite emphasis of the dreams on the brain and its demise.
He also understood dreams as movements of the objective psyche
as reflected so often in the "muddied waters" of the subjective
psyche of the dreamer. That is to say, dreams are first and foremost
movements of the soul as yet implicit (in the background, the
not yet become) but determinative in the sense of catching us in
those movements as they seek materialization or realization in
the world of matter. It therefore makes a huge difference *how*
we participate in those movements emerging out of the forming
future. These hints of the unknown future arrive "clothed" in the
garb of the images we have accumulated from the past, i.e., our
personal unconscious psyche. So, most dreams have a quality of
the unfamiliar appearing in the familiar. In every dream, we sense
something deeply unknown within the images that are familiar
because historical in nature.

David was familiar enough with the current advances in
neuroscience to know that modern consciousness *exists* only
as inextricably linked with the brain and the central nervous
system. Some researchers go as far as claiming to predict what
we think by simply looking at a MRI scan and observing the
section of the brain that "lights up"! David's dreams with their
focus on the brain's demise could therefore be addressing a
soul movement that includes a death of that brain-linked
consciousness.

A death must be undergone! And death is final!

Yet both dreams point to a form of existence in which the
link between consciousness and the brain is severed. The first
dream showed David contemplating his own skull, the skull that
once housed his brain. The second dream explicitly described
David as being "alive but in a very different way".

David then remembered an article he had read in a prominent magazine. The issue was devoted to current research exploring the ties consciousness has to the brain with the predominant conclusion that without the brain, consciousness ceases to exist. The particular article that David remembered was a counter-example to the prevailing wisdom. The author is an orthopaedic surgeon who describes a patient whose brain "had already been destroyed" and yet woke up to say goodbye coherently to his family.

David was next drawn to the disturbing image of meningitis appearing in the dream as an ominous sense of what was to come "next". Meningitis is a disease in which bacteria or virus invade the *meninges*, the membranes that cover and protect the brain tissue. There are three layers: the *pita mater, arachnoid mater* and *dura mater*—tender mother, spider mother, and hard mother. David was jolted when he read this description.

My entire brain, my thinking depends on and is protected by these three aspects of the mother.

This led to further reflective thoughts:

> *Reflective knowledge, i.e., knowledge gained by a consciousness that is separate from everything else is always 'of the past' because reflective. And this knowledge is thus petrified, frozen, not living. Of course, petrifaction and reflection irresistibly invoke the image of the gorgon, Medusa who like the triune meninges of my dream lies behind all such knowledge and its petrifying effect on living process.*

In one of those extraordinary moments that we call synchronicity, David soon after dreamed about petrifaction:

> Early morning in the city, few people around. Some trams sidle into their station, ready to start the day. I drive into a bay. I will follow them. They start off and as I follow the road gets more and more rocky and narrow. Stones become boulders and all my forward motion is impeded. I get anxious and fearful . . .
>
> Then in the city, the broken down part. I see huge cranes lowering long horizontal piece of stone into place. It is an art work called the "Petrified Christ".

As all movement is constricted, hampered, and finally brought to a halt, with fear reaching the level of terror, the ultimate image is displayed, the Petrified Christ. This process was considerably deepened when David received a picture from a friend in response to telling the dream. It is of a carving from fossilised wood of the Pieta, but with a decidedly new twist, appropriately called *New Pieta*.

Carved in fossilized wood (petrifaction), this new Pieta stands
in stark contrast to its predecessors such as Michelangelo's:

David saw straight away that the *New Pieta* shows the mother ineluctably *releasing* her son to the grave where we as observers must follow. We are no longer held by her pity in a kind of suspended condition between life and death. It is the final release from the mother who no longer seeks to protect, holding death's claim at bay.

Death's claim is now absolute!

Similarly David's meninges were now no longer protecting his brain-based consciousness and he was being released to his death. The connection between the knowledge gained by this form of consciousness and the mother whose petrifying stare reduces all living processes to stone lingered with David as he lay quietly in his bed. He began to remember episodes from his own past. He allowed the images to parade before him, as friends might come by for a visit to the departing one. They were shards, fragments, seemingly no longer held together in a contrived continuity by a self-edifying ego. They came in whatever order, or disorder . . .

As they arrived, first in a trickle, David found that he could "ride" one, if he chose, on a basis of attraction or aversion. When that happened, his present state of dying under the tree where he had been placed retreated as if receding down a long tunnel, and he would *become* the memory, reliving its feeling, its consciousness.

And so he "woke up" in a class room:

No! You are wrong! You are all wrong! The forces acting on that object sliding down the inclined plane resolve into these partial forces, not those! I'll prove it to you. I am going to send the entire problem to someone at the University of Queensland and we'll see what he says.

Laughter, Mocking.

Einstein!

Dear John, thank you for sending me this problem on mechanical forces. As you can see from my diagram, your construction is not quite right. The forces rather resolve this way when we place the co-ordinate system on the inclined plane . . . yours sincerely, Dr . . .

Humiliation!

Michael McRobbie. Fat, the butt of many jokes, always trying to belong. I don't mock him. I want to be friends. Why doesn't he come over to my place? I always go to his. He wants to be with Wayne Rubenstein, who always rubbishes him, sparing no pains to humiliate him publically . . .

University of Queensland! I love this place. Physics, Maths, conversations, arguments, study!

Michael, I bet you don't know . . .

Well, Woodcock, all that depends on truth. What is truth, Woodcock?

Silence.

My god, he knows something I do not. He protects himself against the "Rubenstein attacks" with knowledge. He must be studying philosophy. Now I can see how to protect myself against humiliation. I won't be caught off guard again. For starters, I am going to learn a word every day from the dictionary. And, I am going to strengthen my stomach muscles. You can never tell when someone might come at you with a good kick . . .

The shard drifted away and David looked up at the overarching branches of the willow that sheltered him in his last moments.

So that is what I was doing—for so long protecting myself with a carefully constructed edifice of knowledge. Protecting myself from what? Humiliation, mockery! At whose hands? Who stands behind this edifice of knowledge? I have pursued this kind of knowledge for decades, drawing not only from my personal past but the deep past as well.

David then recalled a dream fragment. "You are a Knight Templar" it said. He caught hold of this particular shard and remembered the excitement he felt when he learned that the vows that the Knights Templar took were: Poverty, Chastity and Obedience.

These are my vows! How I lived them during my life!

Further memories of being drawn to junk, cast-off clothes, left-over foods, looking for money in the gutters, dreaming of wealth acquired through finding the 1932 penny that was so rare; strangely shy and modest in all things sexual; first girlfriend while at the University of Queensland; eager to obey authority.

Just tell me what to do!

More shards arrived.

Our past goes further back than the 14th century.

David had engaged with the theory of evolution and its geologic time, aligning himself with those who understood evolution as a simultaneous evolution of consciousness and world. He came to understand that present-day consciousness was simply an outcome and a transformation of former states of consciousness and their correlative world. For example he marvelled at the paintings found in Southern France, over 30 000 years old.

What form of consciousness did we have then?

David could feel the old excitement as he recalled the years of study he had given over to the study of the evolution of consciousness and the world, focussing on what happens to the world when consciousness undergoes a transformation . . .

Now the memories did not have quite such a grip on him. They gathered around his bed under the old willow tree but their hold him was tenuous at best.

He began to realize that these memories were indeed shards. Any meaning they had was an *invested* one.

This must be why we are constantly revising our history texts, our theories of evolution, etc. *Why, we even revise our personal histories under the influence of therapy or education.*

David realized that the meaning-making factor must lie within *us*! When we take up any historical shard, be it personal or geological, any meaning we "find" must have arisen from within us in the first place. So, deep within our almost obessive preoccupation *with* the past and within the myriad self-serving interpretations *of* the past, must be an impulse to come to know the *being* from which we emerged in the form of our modern-day consciousness. Usually a culture favours one interpretation or another and this passes as the "truth". But really this truth is nothing more than an official narrative that serves that culture's need to explain its own origin.

A much more interesting question arose for David. What happens when an individual understands this curious "manufacturing" of meaning? What happens if this individual no longer wishes to favour *any* interpretation of the past.

Let the shards remain shards!

No sooner had these words left David's mouth when a gentle breeze sprung up and began to move the willow branches softly. Like so many leaves, the shards of memories that had gathered around him, as he lay there dying began to tremble and whirl.

As the late afternoon sun broke through the thick canopy, it seemed to resolve itself into a form. David saw a great pair of wings folded forward and eyes that were staring backwards as the light-being, for that surely what it was, began to surge backwards. Its unearthly eyes were fixed on the shards that were gathered there, drawing them together in what became a torrent of glittering light fragments, likewise surging backwards so that angel and shards were moving ever apart, with an increasing velocity, yet the whole scene danced before David's eyes. He heard a dull roar as this catastrophe gained momentum. The angel, moving ever towards the future backwards had its eyes fixed unwaveringly on the shards of the past as its thundering wings beat the torrent into a frothing ever-departing storm wave.

The roar became a cacophany on David's ear and the light gathered in intensity until all he could see was a blinding river of shattered light-forms.

And then, David died.

WORKS CITED

Barfield, O. (1944). *Romanticism Comes of Age*. London: Anthroposophical Press.

_____(1962). *Saving the Appearances: A Study in Idolatry*. London: Faber and Faber.

_____(1965). *Unancestral Voice*. Middletown: Wesleyan University Press.

Batchelor, H. (1996). Gothic Romance. In *Grolier Encyclopedia*. Danbury: Grolier Interactive.

Benjamin, W. (1968). *Illuminations: Essays and Reflections*. (H. Arendt, Ed.) New York: Schocken Books.

Edinger, E. (1984). *The Creation of Consciousness*. Toronto: Inner City.

Giegerich, W. (2001) *The Soul's Logical Life*. Frankfurt: Peter Lang.

_____(2010c). *The Soul Always Thinks*. New Orleans: Spring.

Grimm, J. a. (2007, April 12). *Household Tales*. Retrieved from Wikipedia: http://en.wikipedia.org/wiki/The_Valiant_Little_Tailor

Hillman, J. (1979). Senex and Puer. In C. Giles (Ed.), *Puer Papers*. Irving: Spring Publications Inc.

Iyer, P. (1998, April). Leonard Cohen Unplugged. *The Buzz Magazine*.

Jung, C. G. (1976). *Mysterium Coniunctionus*. Princeton: Princeton University Press.

_____(1980). *The Symbolic Life* (Vol. 18). (R. F. Hull, Trans.) Princeton: Princeton University Press.

_____(1988). *Nietzsche's Zarathustra: Notes of the Seminar given in 1934-1939*. (J. L. Jarrett, Ed.) Princeton: Princeton University Press.

_____(1989). *Memories, Dreams, Reflections.* New York: Vintage Books.

Kingsley, P. (2003). *Reality.* Inverness: Golden Sufi Cente.

Marlowe, S. (1996). *The Lighthouse at the End of the World.* New York: Plume.

Melville, H. (1980). *Moby Dick.* New York: Penguin.

Oliver, M. (1990). *House of Light.* Boston: Beacon Press.

Tarnas, R. (1991). *The Passion of the Western Mind: Understanding the Ideas That Have Shaped Our World.* Reading: Cox and Wyman Ltd.

Woodcock, J. C. (2009). *Transformation of the World.* Bloomington: iUniverse.

_____(2011). *The Imperative.* Bllomingtom: iUniverse, Inc.

_____(2012). *Making of a Man: Initiation Through the Divine Mother* (2nd ed.). Bloomington: iUniverse.

John C. Woodcock holds a doctorate in Consciousness Studies (1999). His thesis articulates the process and outcome of a spiritual ordeal that lasted twenty years. At first it seemed to John that he was undergoing a purely personal psychological crisis but over time, with assistance from his various mentors, he discovered that he was also participating in the historical process of a transformation of the soul as reflected in the enormous changes occurring in our culture, often referred to as apocalyptic.

As these powerful and determinative processes took hold of John's being, his task was at first simply to contain them while somehow carrying on with ordinary life. John's first books, *Living in Uncertainty, Living with Spirit* (the present volume being the second edition); *Making of a Man: Initiation through the Divine Mother*, and *Transformation of the World* describe how he managed to live in a dual reality, since for many years he could not reconcile his inner experience of soul life and external ordinary life.

Over time John began to comprehend how external reality, seemingly so bereft of soul, is indeed itself a manifestation of soul. Soul and world were found to be a unity of differences. This discovery opened up the possibility of discerning soul movement from within present external reality, comprising hints of the unknown future. John's next three books, *The Coming Guest*, *The Imperative*, and *Hearing Voices*, explore this idea more fully by describing the initiatory process and outcome of a human being's becoming a vehicle for the expression of the unknown future, through the medium of his or her art.

John's latest book, *Animal Soul* establishes a firm theoretical ground for the claim that the soul is urging us towards the development of new inner capacities that he calls the augur-artist mind—the mind that can discern and artistically render the hints of the unknown future.

In this updated second edition of *Living in Uncertainty, Living with Spirit* the author gives a more refined definition of the literary art form that the augur-artist mind has taken in his own life.

John currently lives with his wife Anita in Sydney, where he teaches, writes, and consults with others concerning their soul life. He is also a practicing Jungian therapist.

He may be contacted at *jwoodcock@lighthousedownunder.com*